How to Teach *Peace* to Children

Second Edition

Anne Meyer Byler

Herald
Press

Scottdale, Pennsylvania
Waterloo, Ontario

Library of Congress Cataloging-in-Publication Data
Byler, Anne Meyer, 1959-
    How to teach peace to children / Anne Meyer Byler.—2nd ed.
       p. cm.
Includes bibliographical references.
    ISBN 0-8361-9224-9 (pbk. : alk. paper)
    1. Peace—Religious aspects—Christianity—Study and teaching. 2. Christian
education—Home training. I. Title.
    BT736.4 .B95 2002
    248.8'45—dc21

                2002007970

HOW TO TEACH PEACE TO CHILDREN
Copyright © 1981, 2003 by Herald Press, Scottdale, Pa. 15683
    Published simultaneously in Canada by Herald Press,
    Waterloo, Ont. N2L 6H7. All rights reserved
Library of Congress Catalog Number: 2002007970
International Standard Book Number: 0-8361-9224-9
Printed in the United States of America
Book and cover design by Anne Berry

10 09 08 07 06 05 04 03 10 9 8 7 6 5 4 3 2 1

To order or request information, please call
1-800-759-4447 (individuals); 1-800-245-7894 (trade).
Website: www.mph.org

To my family and friends
who are walking this road with me.

Contents

O God,

for too long the world
has called us to war,
and our dead lie sprawled
across the bleeding centuries.

But you

break the bow and shatter the spear,
calling us to sow the seeds of peace
in the midst of despair.

In tenderness,

may we take the tiniest sprouts
and plant them
where they can safely grow
into blossoms of hope. AMEN

—Linea Reimer Geiser

Preface

In 1981, J. Lorne Peachey filled a gap in Christian literature with the first edition of this book. He brought together practical suggestions to help parents pass on peacemaking values, and he gave specific ways the church could help in this task. This edition builds on those suggestions, adding issues that weren't issues then and including references to many other helpful materials.

Peachey clearly identified peacemaking as more than just avoiding conflict. His starting point was the biblical concept of shalom. Peace education in families, he wrote, means "learning the values of reconciliation and problem-solving, of justice and love, of establishing proper relationships without as well as a sense of well-being within." His book has remained in print for over twenty years, and the foundational concept of shalom is as relevant as ever.

Since then, more Christian resources for teaching peace have appeared. These include parenting resources and Sunday school and vacation Bible school curricula with topics ranging from conflict resolution, to appreciation of diversity, to global justice. They come in both book and video formats. The interfaith Institute for Peace and

Justice, founded by Jim and Kathleen McGinnis of the Catholic faith tradition, has continued to present new parenting resources, including a 1990 revision of their classic book *Parenting for Peace and Justice* and the creation of the Families Against Violence Advocacy Network.[1]

Secular educational publishers have also developed materials for parents and teachers on how to teach values like cooperation, respect, and compassion, and how to teach skills like problem solving and mediation. *Raising Peaceful Children in a Violent World* looks at communication, conflict resolution, diversity, sex roles, media and toys, and global issues—with specific family activities and annotated book lists.[2] Other organizations, like Alternatives for Simple Living and Parenting Press, make a broad range of useful resources easily accessible.

Major changes affecting families

Beside the substantial increase in peacemaking resources available to families, other significant changes have affected families in the past twenty years. The growing number of single parents means that more people are shouldering parenting tasks alone. The definition of family continues to change.

Women's career options have increased, and they often find managing work outside and inside the home an increasingly precarious balancing act. Two-career couples face hard choices about vocation, location, finances, and day-to-day nurture of their children. Families working at minimum- or low-wage jobs struggle to make ends meet from paycheck to paycheck, while in North America the gap between those with and those without financial resources grows.[3] In the U.S. particularly, many people on lower incomes live without the safety net of health insurance. Yet many families in both Canada and the U.S. literally buy into a consumer lifestyle, using more than their fair share of the world's resources.

In recent years, the violence hidden in Christian and non-Christian homes was disturbingly revealed as women began to share their painful stories of physical, sexual, and emotional abuse. Differences of opinion continue within the church about the validity of women in congregational leadership roles, becoming a visible justice issue.

Concerns about care for the earth have grown within the church and society. Anti-racism work and diversity training have begun to address issues of systemic racism and white privilege both in the church and out.

In 1980, draft registration became a legal requirement in the U.S. for all eighteen-year-olds, without the option of registering as a conscientious objector. Canada has no such registration. Since 1981, the U.S. continued military interventions around the world—in Panama, the Persian Gulf, Yugoslavia, the "war on drugs" in Colombia, and the wide-ranging "war on terrorism" following the attacks of September 11, 2001. Canada put its military strength behind the war on terrorism as well.

Last, but not least, incredible technological advances have greatly affected families around the world. VCRs and computers have become part of most homes in North America. In the late 1990s, widespread use of the Internet contributed to an information explosion.

The current challenge

Now that material on teaching peace is more available, we face an overwhelming amount of information. How can we find what we need when we need it? This book provides practical information, based on the biblical values of shalom, gathered into one place. It is neither an exhaustive list nor a catalog of activities for every family. It offers an abundance of options to consider for living out peacemaking convictions. As peacemakers, we need to prayerfully decide, each in our own context, where to put our God-given energy, and support others who are doing likewise.

This book addresses issues like the frantic pace of life, rising consumerism, and increasingly graphic violence in toys, videos, and computer games. It also suggests where to find other helpful resources. In addition, the companion website (http://peace.mennolink.org/teachpeace), contains resource lists that you can search by age, subject, and format, and links to other sites that complement the information here. This book and website are for parents who want to help their children become responsible global citizens and, in George Fox's words, "walk lightly on God's earth."

I, with my husband Mark, am in the process of raising three daughters: Maria (14), Rose (12), and Jazzmin (6). This book comes out of that journey. I hope other Christian parents and educators will find *How to Teach Peace to Children* a practical guide, as well as a link to many other useful shalom lifestyle materials.

Chapter 1

Peace

Only a transformation of society so that things are really all right will make for biblical peace.

—Perry B. Yoder[1]

Is peacemaking at the center of a Christian's faith and practice? Or is it an add-on expectation, something only for super Christians to attempt? Is it something we live out as citizens of our country or just as members of our congregation or family? This chapter addresses these questions.

The peace of Christ

At the opening of this twenty-first century, increasing numbers of Christians and whole denominations are asking what Jesus has to teach us today about living the way of peace in a violent world. Lutherans, Presbyterians, and Baptists, among others, have joined the Mennonites, Friends, and Brethren with denominational peacemaking programs that support families in peace education.

Most Christians agree that Jesus was a peacemaker in his life and that he did not resort to violence.[2] He spoke up assertively on behalf of others, accused perpetrators of injustice (even religious leaders), healed the sick, and supported the economic justice of jubilee. Jesus valued the marginal people in Jewish society—women, tax collectors,

> *It is possible to describe the entire ministry of Jesus as a single act of peacemaking: . . . healing of the sick, the feeding of the hungry, the care of the neglected and despised, and the forgiveness of sins—[these] are all aspects of the restoration of God's peace . . . The core is captured in the phrase: Jesus the peacemaker.*
>
> —Ulrich Mauser

and the sick. He told his followers to love their enemies and to put down their swords. Many fewer Christians today, however, will go on to say that this is the way Jesus' followers should strive to live today.

But Jesus' description of peacemaking in the Sermon on the Mount is not an impossible ideal. Why would he share the impossible with the crowds that flocked to hear him? It is rather very good news for people weary of violence and longing for another way. Jesus, living in an oppressed society of the first century, was a flesh-and-blood peacemaking example of nonviolent resistance to evil. His instructions to "love your enemies" and "turn the other cheek" are also a call for Christians today.[3] Like the Ten Commandments, they are not suggestions to take or leave, but guidelines for living that are within our grasp through the grace of the Holy Spirit and the power of the resurrection.

Finally, Jesus' peacemaking lifestyle was not a solo venture. Jesus chose twelve special friends to accompany him until the end. And, uncharacteristic in that day, women, too, were recorded among his followers. He spent time with his good friends from Bethany: Mary, Martha, and Lazarus. The post-resurrection New Testament story tells of communities in Jerusalem, Antioch, Rome, and elsewhere who prayed and worshiped together, encouraged each other, shared tasks, and saw to each other's financial and physical needs. So too with peacemakers of today, including—and perhaps even particularly—peacemaking parents. We need the same fellowship, challenge, shared modeling, and encouragement of a faith community.

Shalom

The word *shalom* in the Hebrew Old Testament carries a deeper meaning than the English translation, *peace*. It involves healing, reconciliation, wholeness, and completeness. When shalom appears in the Old Testament it may be translated into English as peace, but is also translated as *well, favorable*, and *rest assured*. The New Testament Greek term *eirene* carries a meaning just as rich, reflecting a transformation toward wholeness in the relationship between God and God's people, as well as between people.[4]

Biblical shalom involves all levels of life: personal, family, community, and global. This lived Christianity is not only for our homes and congregations, with different rules at work or on the school playground. What is our testimony if we preach and practice shalom in church and with those in our town, but then support violent retaliation when another country attacks ours? If Jesus did not fragment his life in this way, why would we, who claim him as inspiration and leader? Rather, we strive to follow the Jesus who lived a shalom lifestyle.

Shalom brings our whole lives before God. Consider that Jesus, at all times beside us to guide and direct us, observes our interactions with others. (At times, I've been embarrassed to think of Jesus—or any adult, for that matter—hearing the way I addressed my children.)

Shalom is relevant to many issues of contemporary life. It values:

- the lives of the unborn—promoting adoption over abortion,
- those on the margins—advocating for children, people without financial resources, and those with disabilities,
- people in other countries, even those labeled enemies—promoting nonmilitary responses in conflict,
- those who have committed crimes—rejecting the death penalty, and
- the dignity of those who disagree with us— using respectful language.[5]

In 1983, a committee of U.S. Roman Catholic bishops, chaired by Cardinal Bernardin, drafted the document *The Challenge of Peace: God's Promise and Our Response*. They called for nuclear disarmament, linking the issue to their longstanding opposition to abortion.[6] Bernardin described this consistent pro-life ethic as "the seamless garment."

God's shalom speaks to every aspect of our personal lives and our world today, as it did in Jesus' life and in his world. "Blessed are the peacemakers," Jesus said in Matthew 5:9, "for they will be called the children of God." Jesus chose the way of nonviolence to achieve his goals. As a Christian parent, I want to follow Jesus, the Prince of Peace.

Discussion questions:

1. Are there parts of your life (at home, at work, at church) where you are embarrassed to think of Jesus witnessing your interactions? Which parts? What makes you feel that way?
2. Are aspects of a "consistent pro-life ethic" hard for you to support whole-heartedly? Which ones? How might you work at these growing edges in your life?
3. If Jesus came today, what parts of society might he find most in need of the holistic peace with justice that characterizes shalom?
4. What aspects of your current life nurture your own sense of shalom?

Chapter 2

Families

> If we are to reach real peace in this world, and if we are to carry on a real war against war, we shall have to begin with children.
>
> —Mahatma Gandhi[1]

Today's families

Families have changed in the last twenty years, but they still have a major impact on children's lives. The new challenges described in the introduction have inspired new ways of living faithfully. Godparents, extended family members, and adopted aunts, uncles, and grandparents can fill an important role for children, modeling concern for people and creation. They also provide companionship and support for parents. Mentors in the church family can create intentional relationships with children.

In blended families, parents can model respect and communication skills as they work out issues with former spouses. Men and women with living wage job options and creativity can break out of the sixty-hour work week mold and choose work that lets them spend time with their children. Some men are taking on the role of primary caregiver during their children's formative years. Courageous women are accepting God's call to use their gifts in ministry and leadership.

The role of modeling *and* explanation

How does biblical shalom, whole peace, relate to parenting today? To be people of integrity, we must bring this vision of peace home, in actions and in words. Robert Coles, a psychologist who did extensive research into moral development, writes:

> "Prior to a particular time of crisis or concern we have all along been making certain moral points to our children, sending them messages directly or by implication: our notion of how one ought to behave under a variety of circumstances."[2]

The old adage says actions speak louder than words, but a recent study shows that words may be just as important in passing on beliefs and values. Lynn Okagaki, in child development and family studies at Purdue University, reported, "Regular, specific conversations about religious beliefs . . . gave students more accurate perceptions of what their parents actually believe. It's not enough for parents to just model beliefs for their kids."[3] Both modeling and explaining your beliefs about shalom are important in passing them on to your children.

Talking about beliefs and values

Since explaining your beliefs may seem harder than modeling them, here are some ideas to get you started:

1. **Don't assume your children know what you believe** or why you do something, even if you've told them already. (Think how many times you need to tell them to hang up their coats!)

2. **Talk about faith issues with your children.** Openly discuss the values behind decisions you make. When a tough situation comes up in your family or in the world, put meaning back into an overly-used phrase by discussing "What *would* Jesus do?" Talk about your first allegiance being to God. When might friends or our government ask us to violate God's laws? Discuss biblical events and other historical situations where God's people have decided to follow God's leading rather than the government's demands.

3. **Let non-conforming, peacemaking actions be a springboard for discussion.** When my husband, Mark, felt an uncharacteristic, sudden urge to go with Christian Peacemaker Teams to the island of Vieques, Puerto Rico, he believed God was calling him. He felt good about standing with those who protested peacefully against the U.S. military's training exercises on their island. The third time Mark went to Vieques, he was arrested. To help our four-year-old understand this, we told her about others—from Paul and Silas to Martin Luther King Jr.—who were put in jail for helping others. Jazzmin ended up making valentines for those who were dropping the bombs, hoping this might make them want to stop.

Children grow toward peace as they live with persons who practice and interpret the spirit of Christ.

—Kathryn Aschliman

4. **Talk about your everyday actions.** Why do you read the magazines you do? Why do you serve on certain committees? Why do you recycle? Why are you involved with church and service activities when you could be doing something else?

5. **Read stories together** about people living out shalom values. *Peace Begins with You* wonderfully summarizes many aspects of shalom-type peace for younger elementary children: having what you need and some of what you want, being allowed to be different, and caring about peace for others and the earth. *Raising Peaceful Children in a Violent World* has a chapter "Peaceful Literature: Finding Role Models for Peace in Children's Books" that shares documented benefits from reading, ways to choose literature, and a number of recommended books and related activities.[4]

Since books are a strong ally in nurturing peacemakers, I mention many titles throughout these chapters. In addition, a much longer, annotated peace resource list and links to many other lists are available at the companion website (http://peace.mennolink.org/teachpeace). *You do not need to buy these books to take advantage of them.* Most libraries offer inter-library loan, letting you borrow almost any title, even out-of-print ones, from other participating libraries. If you do wish to purchase a book, many online used book services offer good deals.

Read with your children about nonviolent efforts to solve conflicts and how environmentalists have cared for the earth. Read about strong, resourceful girls and thoughtful, sensitive boys. Learn about the many cultures in your country and the world. Be willing to learn hard truths about how peoples have been mistreated, at home and abroad, by governments and church institutions.

6. **Keep a sense of humor.** The present world is sometimes so far from what God intends that it is easy to get discouraged. When it seems few Christians are even taking seriously the words and actions of their chosen leader, we might find it hard to live in joyful obedience. But the alternative—a heavy, duty-driven life—is hardly appealing to anyone, least of all our children!

In the spring of 2002, amid suicide bombings and Israeli attacks on refugee camps, Pax Christi invited people to light two candles in their homes, one for Israelis and one for Palestinians. We did this at suppertime when we remembered. The first time, a small, colored feather remained on the table from some craft project. One of the girls asked, "What's the feather for?" "For the chickens," I impulsively answered. Mark took off on the idea and said, "You can imagine how hard it is to lay eggs when bombs are going off, tanks are coming through, and soldiers are shooting."

Dealing with unrealistic expectations and failure

"What do you expect me to be?" my daughter yelled. "Perfect?!" Well, no, I didn't think so, just reasonable. She obviously felt my standards for her were too high. Sometimes we find that our standards for ourselves are too high.

Those of us who are too hard on ourselves stray easily into a legalism toward others and ourselves that is not from God. Then ideas or values get in the way of loving actions. A friend shared an incident with her daughter:

> When Amanda was learning to bake, she had a book from the library and tried a recipe. She thought it was perfect. It looked

just like the picture in the book. "You should have used a little whole wheat flour," I told her. I didn't realize until much later how disappointed she felt. She'd created this wonderful bread, and then Mom responded with criticism.

Using whole wheat may be important, but it's not as important as affirming positively the beauty your child has created.

Since failure and frustration are a part of everyones' lives, those of us wanting to prepare our children to live full lives need to share with them how to handle failure in themselves and others in a *good* way (and all this perhaps while even learning it ourselves). This is a part of inner peace and relational peace that dedicated peacemakers sometimes lose sight of. Jesus' high calling can contribute to constant disappointment or to a reliance on God's grace through confession, humility, and forgiveness that empowers and brings joy.[5]

A shalom lifestyle

In 1980, Doris Longacre, author of *More-with-Less Cookbook* and *Living More with Less*, listed actions of shalom living that go beyond first-glance peacemaking. Her five more-with-less standards of voluntary simplicity in a complicated world summarize shalom living:

- Do justice.
- Learn from the world community.
- Nurture people (not things).
- Cherish the natural order (care for all creation).
- Nonconform freely. [6]

Today's world brings new challenges for families who want to live in peace with God, neighbors near and far, and God's creation. Ways to value all of life and live those values are at the core of this book. The following chapters deal with specific issues in peace-and-justice parenting.

Discussion questions:

1. How has your congregation experienced and addressed changes in family life over the years?
2. How did your family of origin model and talk about shalom values? What from this are you trying to retain? What would you like to change in your own family?
3. How do you typically respond to failure in living out your ideals?
4. What discussions have you had with your children about shalom values (like those expressed by Doris Longacre)? What discussions would you like to have?

Chapter 3

Shalom Living: Relationships

> *The relation between God and the people of faith . . . provides the basis for our understanding of God. Our knowledge of God comes mainly from this relationship and its history.*
>
> —Confession of Faith in a Mennonite Perspective[1]

Our God is a relational God. As people touched by, and committed to, God's transforming love, we choose to interact "according to the likeness of God." The history of God's faithfulness and love—and God's nonviolent love in Jesus—shows us the way to relate to each other as God's children.[2]

1. Nurture your marriage and other adult relationships.

If we want to live at peace with others, it is essential that we tend our marriages and relationships with other adults. Psychologist Becky Bailey notes, "Husbands and wives battle with each other, using attack skills like name-calling and withdrawal. Then they demand that their children resolve conflicts calmly, by discussing them."[3]

Your children see the way you and your spouse, former spouse, and other significant adults in your life relate to each other. Do you speak respectfully, demonstrate your love, and affirm each other? How do you share household tasks? Do you discuss household issues that concern both of you, like finances? How do you speak about people at church or work with whom you disagree?[4]

With less time at home and complex children's schedules, it's hard for busy marriage partners to find time to address important issues.

This lets smaller issues grow into larger issues that can cause major problems. Marriages need quality time and nurture, the same as children. If you can't seem to find a satisfactory resolution to nagging problems, go to a counselor sooner rather than later. Asking for help is a sign of maturity and a good example for children. Ask your pastors to recommend people who are experienced in helping couples work out issues and deepen their relationships.[5]

2. Discipline: Think through the messages you are sending.

Healthy relationships have many facets, including communication, respect, caring, and boundaries. We may want to treat our children respectfully and not humiliate them, but find ourselves falling back into unhelpful patterns. Books in the "Developing Capable People" series are useful—*Positive Discipline* looks at counter-productive forms of discipline.[6] *The Peaceful Parenting Handbook* also provides discipline strategies to help address childhood behavior problems in a peaceful way before they get out of hand. *Raising Peaceful Children in a Violent World* has a chapter on peace-compatible discipline strategies.[7]

Anger. Unfortunately, not dealing appropriately with anger makes things worse in the long run. Dealing with anger in a good way, however, is hard work. I remember my exasperation and surprise when, after a loud string of stubborn retorts from my daughter, I yelled, "You are going to *have* to stop yelling!" Acknowledging our own anger and enabling our children to do the same is a good place to start.

Dr. James Dobson wrote that the most common error in disciplining children is "the inappropriate use of anger in attempting to manage boys and girls. It is one of the most ineffective methods . . . Adult anger incites a malignant kind of disrespect in their minds." He encourages disciplinary action that your children will care about. "Then administer it with 'cool.'"[8]

Spanking/hitting. Anger as a prime motivator is one of my objections to spanking. Spanking, even as a last resort, comes quicker whenever the parent is angry, stressed, and out of other ideas. But the basic message it sends about conflict is also troubling: when you run out of ideas and people are being their worst, then it is okay to hurt them to make them stop. Astrid Lindgren presents a thought-provoking situation:

> When I was about twenty years old, I met an old pastor's wife who told me that when she was young and had her first child, she didn't believe in striking children, although spanking kids with a switch pulled from a tree was standard punishment at the time. But one day when her son was four or five, he did something that she felt warranted a spanking—the first of his life. And she told him that he would have to go outside and find a switch for her to hit him with.
>
> The boy was gone a long time. When he came back in, he was crying. He said to her, "Mama, I couldn't find a switch, but here's a rock you can throw at me."
>
> All of a sudden the mother understood how the situation felt from the child's point of view: If my mother wants to hurt me, then it makes no difference what she does it with. She might as well do it with a stone.[9]

I'll readily acknowledge the extremely frustrating nature of some children's behavior and the feeling that nothing will convey its inappropriateness as well as a spanking, yet the violence and inconsistency related to spanking remain.

3. Give your child a positive framework for understanding conflicts and angry feelings.

Conflict (any situation where people disagree and it bothers one of them) is a normal part of life. So is its frequent companion—angry feelings. It's not something to avoid, as those who work in conflict transformation have taught for decades. Paul wrote to the Christians at Ephesus: "Be angry but do not sin."[10] Jesus also got angry at injustice.[11] But conflict still makes people uncomfortable, causing many families and congregations to shy away from it.

In families, it's best to acknowledge people's feelings—whatever they are. The feelings are okay. Not all responses are okay, however. Help your child identify and work through angry feelings in a positive way.[12]

For instance, you might say, "I see your lip is sticking out, Ben. It looks like you're angry. Are you mad at Elena for stepping on your toy?" Or perhaps, "It's okay to be angry when someone messes with your stuff. But it's *not* okay to hit her. That hurts. What else could you do about it?" You might directly address ways to cope with angry feelings: "You seem *really* angry and I can understand why . . . (Let your child talk about the feelings) . . . Do you want some ideas of what to do with those feelings that won't hurt anybody?" Running outside, kicking a ball, talking to someone about it, writing about it, and hitting the bed are some options.[13]

In a conflict, certain words and actions escalate the problem; others scale it down. Teasing, blaming, name-calling, bringing up past problems, generalizing ("you *always* or *never* . . ."), and ridiculing tend to escalate the conflict. Acknowledging the other person's point of view, humor (but not at the other person's expense), using a calm voice, and suggesting a compromise help reduce the conflict. Even younger children can understand this concept since they are usually entranced by escalators when they encounter them in stores.

4. Help your child understand responses to conflict and choose appropriate options.

Brainstorming with children the wide-ranging options available to parties in a conflict is useful, stretching young imaginations to envision new possibilities. But it is also important for children to understand that different personalities tend to react differently to conflict. Some people clam up and try to leave the room as quickly as possible. Others jump in with both feet and loud opinions, while others are more laid back. Understanding this can comfort children who often find themselves in the middle of the fray with both fists up. This list, with animals representing five basic responses, can help children:

- SHARK—a forcing, win-lose style
- TEDDY BEAR—giving in
- TURTLE—avoiding or leaving
- FOX—compromising or meeting half-way
- OWL—problem solving, or win-win

For older children, the grid below shows when they are the most useful. One direction measures the importance of the relationship, the other, the importance of the issue.

For example, when you and a good friend are deciding what movie to see, and you really don't care, it makes sense to be a teddy bear and give in, because the relationship is important, but the issue is not. On the other hand, the shark, or forcing response, makes sense if friends are trying to convince you to shoplift something, because the issue, or doing the right thing, is more important than the relationship. If an obnoxious salesperson wants to sell you a coat you don't want, leaving, the turtle response, might be best, since neither the issue nor the relationship is that important.

In a family situation, however, with people you care about and with an issue that's bound to come up again, avoiding conflict isn't usually helpful in the long run. The problem solving, or owl response isn't *always* the best one, but it's one we want to develop for frequent use in our relationships.

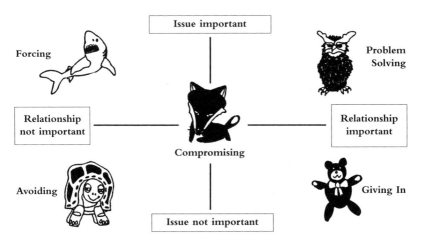

The companion website (http://peace.mennolink.org/teachpeace) offers a tool to help children and adults determine their most comfortable way(s) of responding and then help them reflect on that information.[14]

5. Teach your children healthy ways to work through conflict (and follow them yourself!).

Present ground rules for fighting fair:

- Use "I" messages (not "You make me so angry when . . ." but "I feel angry when . . . ")
- Identify and focus on the problem.
- Attack the problem, not the person.
- Listen with an open mind; rephrase.
- Treat the other person's feelings with respect.
- Take responsibility for your actions.
- Don't intimidate with size or power.

(These were developed for school-age children by Fran Schmidt and Alice Friedman.[15] The final point is my own.)

Of course, the same rules help in conflicts between parents and children. Even when parents are trying to be reasonable, they sometimes resort to an exasperated or sarcastic tone. My daughters report that this comes across as threatening or yelling, even without the volume!

These points are good ground rules for anyone who wants to work at resolving a conflict. In addition, these steps are also useful in working through a conflict, with or without a third party:

- Take turns telling what happened, without interruption.
- Make sure each party understands statements *and* feelings shared. Rephrase if necessary.
- Brainstorm possible solutions.
- Choose the solution(s) each party is willing to live with.
- Find the one solution most agreeable to each.
- If necessary, set up a time in the future to evaluate the solution.

Don't underestimate children's abilities to brainstorm creatively. My daughter, in kindergarten, was arguing with a friend about who should sit in the front seat on rides to and from school. When I asked for their ideas, Jazzmin suggested that they *both* sit in front! She would sit in the middle of the bench seat and everyone would even be in seat belts. The option hadn't even occurred to me.

Some families have a particular place, like a peace table,[16] where members can go when having a conflict. They must be willing to fight fair and to work toward a solution. If they have trouble taking turns talking, the one talking could hold a "peace stick" (or pencil), giving it to the other when through. Sometimes the parent may need to be present. Other times, people need a cooling off period before such a discussion.

As a parent, remember that the act of working through conflicts can lead to significant personal learning and growth in children. You short-circuit this valuable learning process by legislating solutions: "Why can't you two learn to share? Sandy, you play with it for five minutes and then I'll give it to Chris."[17]

> *Our purpose is not to do away with all quarrels among children . . . Our job seems to be . . . to provide them with creative ways to get out of the holes they dig for themselves. The best present I know to give a child is a good shovel.*
>
> — Linda Crawford

6. Specific tips for parents in conflict with a child:

- Don't get engaged with your child's complaints or actions and end up in a heated argument or shouting match. Stick to facts and state them calmly. (Try envisioning yourself as an observer to the situation, asking what the best course of action is to achieve the desired results.)
- When you get to the end of your rope, take a break if the children aren't on the verge of violence. Go to your bedroom and shut the

door. Call a friend who will understand what you are going through and support you.

- Whenever possible, refrain from legislating solutions—children learn necessary skills when they work toward a solution.
- Admit it when you're wrong. Apologize and say you're sorry.

With children, there are times when you may feel you are reacting appropriately, but the behavior continues. Once, Mark and I decided to give *ourselves* points (1 to 4, depending on how big the conflict and how well we responded) for *our* handling of incidents. Some friends, in a similar parenting situation, did this too. After one couple earned ten points, we got a sitter and went out to eat!

Years later, I kept my cool with my daughter in the grocery store. Afterwards I thought, "That was worth *ten* points all by itself! I'll have to tell Mark." If, in response, I had hit her bottom or hand (or anywhere else), either then or later at home, the message would have been, "*You* may not hit others because it hurts, but parents may."

If, over time, a conflict with your child isn't getting resolved, consider checking with a professional about that behavior. They may have valuable new insights. They may also recognize a chemical problem. Attention deficit and hyperactivity may not respond well to other typical discipline strategies like time out or seclusion. One set of parents tried behavior therapy for a couple of years. A diagnosis of depression and appropriate medication made an amazing difference in this child's life—and his parents'.[18]

7. Prepare your children for conflicts away from home.

Children must also deal with conflict when parents or attentive adults are not present and where the same ground rules and values may not be shared. Listen to your children when they are concerned about these situations. Think together about ways to respond, and pray about it.

A welcoming and non-critical stance toward information your children share will make them more comfortable in confiding such situations to you. To guard against instances where an abusive party may bind them to secrecy, tell your children that the only good secret is one where they know exactly when it will be told (a birthday, when someone comes to visit, etc.). Secrets that are okay *don't* last forever.

Bullying is a perennial problem, particularly in school settings. Victims are hesitant to tell an adult, either because of threats or because they don't want to admit to anyone what is going on. Let your child know that if he is in trouble, you can help keep him safe if he tells you about it. While we tend to think of boys when we think of bullying behavior, the same phenomenon is present among girls as well, though it often takes different forms.

Towards Bully-Free Schools gives details on bully and victim characteristics and typical behavior, along with ideas for effective response. *Odd Girl Out* addresses feminine forms of bullying and anti-social behavior, exploring indirect aggression that may result from the lack of cultural permission for girls to acknowledge conflict or express anger. The author offers strategies for addressing this with your daughters.[19]

Discussion questions:

1. (*Silently*) If you're married, rate the well-being of your relationship with your spouse, on a scale of 1-10. If you're not married, rate the well-being of your relationship with your closest friend or a colleague at work. Think about an issue you'd most like to discuss with that person. (This can be a barometer for how you are currently modeling healthy relationships in your home.)
2. How is getting help for a relationship problem the same as going to a doctor for a physical problem? How is it different?
3. If you're willing, share about a time a third party helped you and another person work through an interpersonal relationship issue.
4. What has your view of conflict and anger in the Christian life been? How does this view fit with biblical perspectives? Is this the view you want to pass on to your children? Why or why not?
5. What typically escalates conflict in your family? What ways to reduce it would you like to use more often?

6. Which fighting fair ground rules do you find most difficult to follow?

7. Can you share a time when your children worked through a conflict well using the suggested steps (or any other process)?

Chapter 4
Shalom Living: Day by Day

> *Whatever enhances the well-being of the human family is peacemaking, the spreading of shalom.*
>
> —Robert McAfee Brown[1]

PACE OF LIFE

Busyness, and the stresses that result, reflects some of the most unpeaceful aspects of contemporary life. Irritability from the pressures of too many demands, tiredness from sleep deprivation, and heart disease are side effects that we suffer when we take on more than God expects us to. An activity level that isn't healthy for us or our families says to the world that we follow a God who is a taskmaster—or that we aren't listening to God or obeying God. Parker Palmer labels this "functional atheism."

1. Keep a day of rest.

Following God's command for Sabbath-keeping improves your psychological health and physical well-being, both necessary for true shalom. "We can change society by beginning a quiet revolution of change in ourselves and our families," says Wayne Muller. "Let us take a collective breath, rest, pray, meditate, walk, sing, eat, and take time to share the unhurried company of those we love."[2] Those with work

> *To allow oneself to be carried away by a multitude of conflicting concerns, to surrender to too many demands, to commit oneself to too many projects . . . is to succumb to violence . . . The frenzy of the activist neutralizes his work for peace. It destroys his own capacity for inner peace.*
>
> —Thomas Merton

commitments on Sunday must set aside other days and times during the week for rest and refreshment.

2. Schedule time to be alone with God.

Find time to sit and learn what is on *God's* agenda for your day. While I am not a get-up-early-before-the-kids person, I have at different times spent ten to fifteen minutes of each day's first "kid-free" time with Scripture, prayer, and/or devotional readings. A friend told me how she got up before her young daughter to have time for prayer and meditation: "My daughter learned that if she came into the living room and found me sitting in my praying chair, she was welcome to quietly sit on my lap, but she wasn't to interrupt me." Many years later, the daughter shared what a comfort it was for her to consistently see her mother in prayer.

3. Pay attention to time commitments.

Think through your priorities. Are they reflected in how you spend your time? Decide what causes and activities are really yours for a given year. If you take on a new committee or task, try to remove another one that's less important.

Set limits for younger children's activities, depending on their energy level and the time they need at home for schoolwork, chores, and unstructured play. Perhaps allow only one or two extra-curricular activities at a time. Think through time commitments with your older children.

4. Build worship and prayer into your family's life.

Add variety to your family mealtime grace. For example, take turns saying one thing you're thankful for, ending with, "Right?" Everyone else responds with, "Right!" Or have each one say something he or she is thankful for, putting a hand into the center of the table afterward. At the end, everyone says "Amen!" and raises their hands out from the center. (Or you can combine these.) The appendix to *Parent Trek* includes sung graces. Graces from many traditions are artistically penned in *One Hundred Graces*.[3]

When you know of a particular concern (a loved one who is traveling or sick, an area of the world in conflict, a big decision, or an event in your congregation) light a special candle before the meal to serve as a reminder that you are holding that concern up for God's loving care. One family has a world map in their kitchen. As they pray for particular people and places in the world, they mark the place on the map.[4]

HOUSEHOLD BUSINESS

When our daughter Maria was seven and Rose was five, we talked with them about "cleaning up our own messes." One morning at breakfast, Maria knocked over a full box of cereal. I said it was okay, but that she needed to pick up the scattered cereal. After a while she said, "Mom, I think you ought to pick them up." "Why?" I asked. "Because you *bought* them!"

We all tend to shirk responsibility when it means work. Obviously, parents can help children in larger tasks, like picking up cereal from all over the kitchen, but we want our children to learn to do for themselves. They can take part in household tasks at a fairly young age. Since it doesn't always save time or seem simpler, you need to decide how important it is to you to involve your children in household chores and which chores to have them do at what ages.

5. Be clear about expectations in sharing household work.

When you want children to take on tasks, work out a household job-sharing plan. Consult resources to find age-appropriate tasks for children and set a time to talk about incorporating them into a weekly plan.[5] Revise and update arrangements periodically as children grow older and people tire of certain tasks.

	Mon	Tues	Wed	Thurs	Fri	Sat	Sun
Make meal	Rose	Mark	Anne	Anne	Mark	Maria	Anne
Set table	Anne	Maria	Rose	Mark	Rose	Mark	Rose
Clear/wash	Maria	Anne	Maria	Rose	Maria	Anne	Mark
Dishwasher	Mark	Rose	Mark	Maria	Anne	Rose	Maria

A chart like the one above can also make clear who is responsible for other tasks: weekly cleaning, after-school responsibilities, or family devotions. It's also helpful to be equally clear about consequences for tasks that are not completed or otherwise negotiated ahead of time.

6. Discuss major concerns that affect everyone.

Various resources elaborate on the family meeting idea.[6] Suggestions include having regularly scheduled meetings and agreeing on rules in advance (like anyone can list an agenda item, everyone may speak freely, and decisions are made by consensus). You might have a sheet of paper where anyone may write an issue they want to discuss. Our family has a blackboard in the kitchen, and we know that's the place to write things we want to talk about. When something is on the board, we discuss it over supper. "Lock for bedroom door!" and "Folding clothes" are two examples of items that have appeared on the blackboard.

Incorporate children into the meeting from start to finish. You might begin with a sharing time or include some particularly fun aspects. Here's a true story from the McGinnis family:

"I can't stand living with him. I can't find anything that's mine. He's always touching my things. I'm so mad, I'm gonna . . . I'm gonna . . . I'm gonna write it on the agenda!" So screamed ten-year-old David as he stormed around the room he shared with his brother Tom . . . David stomped downstairs into the breakfast room where he grabbed a marker pen and wrote in huge letters on a piece of paper posted on the wall, "TOMMY! NOW!" This was David's way of calling for an emergency family meeting.[7]

> *A lantern shows only the next step—not several steps ahead . . . If only the next step is clear, the one thing to do is take it!*
>
> —Amy Carmichael

MONEY MATTERS

Wealth was certainly high on Jesus' agenda: he addressed it more than any other topic except for the kingdom of heaven. He even linked our giving to others to our giving to him when he said, "Just as you did it to one of the least of these . . . you did it to me." Even more striking, "as you did not do to one of the least of these, you did not do it to me."[8]

What does money have to do with peace? To start, money can help assure the basic health and well-being (shalom) of our neighbors. In addition, our desire for more and more can feed conflicts within ourselves and our families.

In the Bible, the responsibility of those with more than enough is clear. People who quote Jesus' "the poor shall be with you always" (Matt. 26:11) as an excuse *not* to give, need to read further in Deuteronomy 15:11, the passage Jesus was likely quoting from. "Since there will never cease to be some in need on the earth, I therefore command you, 'Open your hand to the poor and needy neighbor in your land.'" The Old

- 20% of the world's 6 billion people live in absolute poverty on less than $1/day. 50% live on less than $2/day.

- The income gap between the richest 20% and poorest 20% increased from 30 to 1 in 1960 to 74 to 1 in 1997.

- The wealthiest 20% consume 86% of goods and services, while the poorest 20% consume 1.3%.[9]

Testament's year of remission or year of jubilee was designed to regularly redistribute assets that grew uneven with time.[10]

7. Be clear that all we have comes from God.

We need to be up front with our children that all we have—our bodies, skills, possessions, income—comes from God. Our wealth is not ours alone, since we had nothing to do with the family or country or economic class we were born into. Talk about how those of us with much more than the basics might respond to needs around us. When we share, are we only benefiting others?[11]

8. Guard against consumerism.

Talk with your children about how few people in the world—perhaps one in five or six—own the kinds of appliances and toys your family does. Check out the fascinating book, *The Material World*, and see what household goods are typical in other countries. Talk with your children about how the goals of marketing and advertising (getting as many people as possible to buy the product) may not fit with your family's goals.[12]

Stores display attractive merchandise close to children's eye level. Use this guideline with younger children when in stores: "'I like it, I like it, I like it!' is fine. 'I want it, I want it, I want it!' is not fine. This helps children learn that they may like as much as they want, but they don't have to own everything they like."[13]

> *There are two ways to get enough. One is to continue to accumulate more and more. The other is to desire less.*
> —G. K. Chesterton

9. Keep track of family spending.

Record-keeping software or workbooks are available for this. Consider getting together at the end of the year with other adults. We've done this with both close friends who shared our values and with siblings and their spouses. Share about how you spent money, how you feel about it, and what you'd like to change. Let your children know that you are doing this and why.

10. Give a "graduated tithe" to your church and other organizations. Encourage your children to tithe.

Ron Sider, in his first edition of *Rich Christians in an Age of Hunger*, had a forthright discussion of a graduated tithe.[14] His family decided to give away ten percent of their income up to a subsistence level—what it would take to live with few luxuries. They settled this at several thousand over "poverty level," which for a family of four in 2002 comes to $18,100.[15] Then they gave a greater percent of increments above that. Let your children choose where to give part of this amount. Encourage them to set apart a tithe from their own earnings or allowance.

> ### A graduated tithe in 2002[16]
>
> A family of four might give 10% of its income up to an elevated poverty level of $25,000. You might then give 15% of the next $3,000, 20% of the next $3,000 and so on. If you made $40,000 a year, you'd be giving $6,250 (16%) to the church and other charities. At $79,000, you'd be giving $33,550 (42%) and living on $45,450. Above that, you'd give away everything you earned.

HAPPY, HOLY HOLIDAYS

Celebrations are certainly a valuable part of a full family life. Just as festivals and feasts played a large role in the life of God's people throughout the Bible, gatherings—whether for birthdays, potlucks, holidays, or game nights—offer our families a wealth of memories.

Our behavior during our celebrations, including religious holidays, demonstrates our response to the Bible's message about wealth. Think about the kind of life Jesus lived. How would you describe Jesus' life message in one sentence? Now think about our society's celebration of Christmas—Jesus' birthday. What is the message we hear? How do you spend your time and money for Jesus' birthday? Are there any changes you might hope to make in next year's celebration?[17]

I find it easiest to just stay away from large stores at Christmas time. When I do go in and there are Salvation Army collection pots outside, I tax myself a dollar each time, letting one of my children put it in the kettle. Here are some other ways to keep our message in line with Jesus' message at this time of year.

11. Give less to those who already have too much.

Exchanging names rather than buying for all family members is one way to give less to those who have too much. Your family might agree to give only homemade items, garage sale items, or white elephants from your house. Or set a price limit.

Circulate wish lists among family members. This takes the guesswork out of gift giving and also enables people to share something that they aren't using anymore with someone who can use it. The lists don't have to be completely serious, either. Our lists have included: neat decorative thingies that can make a dorm room a more cozy place, your favorite cookbook, dress-up clothes, a couple of weeks of days with thirty hours in them, dark chocolate in any form, a back rub, and an airplane—complete with pilot's license.

Consider making give lists with your children instead of wish lists. During Advent, help them think of specific items family members and friends would enjoy, and write them down.[18]

12. Give more to those who have less.

Contribute money you would have spent buying expensive gifts to organizations like the Mennonite Central Committee, Habitat for Humanity, or Heifer Project International.[19] For the latter, see how much money your family can raise, and let the youngest generation choose which animals to buy. Our family brings three generations together at the holidays, so we decided one year that the first and second generations would match whatever the third generation (fifteen grandchildren, age three months to twenty one years) donated. Together we bought a water buffalo, a goat, and some chicks!

13. Give creative gifts.

For birthdays or Father's or Mother's Day, make a book about the person with younger children. Call it something like *Grandpa Likes . . .* or *Aunt Marjory at 47*. Color the pages and add commentary. For younger children's birthdays, put together a birthday kit. (Wrap each item for more surprises.) This could include items for playing office (Post-It notes, a receipt book, a small memo pad, colored pens), doctor (Band-Aids and cloth wrap, patient registration forms, and name tags), or baker (homemade playdough, cookie cutters, and little plates).[20]

SERVICE LEARNING

With stark inequalities in our nations, there are plenty of opportunities to address these inequalities and bring shalom. Responses that build shalom go beyond giving money to organizations. And, while we may have things to offer, we will all gain more if we go with a learner's stance.

14. Contribute to physical needs beyond your family.

Teens and parents could serve with Mennonite Disaster Service. Your local Red Cross might have programs you could participate in as a family. If there is a local chapter, take your older children with you to help build a Habitat for Humanity house.[21] Such activities help children make tangible connections with people making do with much less. To encourage local connections, make food for a local homeless shelter—better yet, take the food and join the residents for supper.

To act on beliefs in the sanctity of life of the unborn, provide support for girls and women with unplanned pregnancies who would otherwise be going it alone. Get involved financially or relationally, depending on the programs available in your community. Consider foster parenting or adoption. This provides a family for children born to people unable or unwilling to give them the home they deserve.

15. Advocate on behalf of others.

Mennonite Central Committee (MCC) has action alerts for letter writing campaigns and information on many topics—hunger, military spending, and particular geographic regions of the world. It also has many educational resources. American Friends Service Committee (AFSC) and the Friends Committee on National Legislation (FCNL) have other programs and resources.[22]

MARGINALIZED PEOPLE AND CULTURES

North America is a continent of immigrants. Most of us living here have ancestors who were immigrants. It's important to explore this aspect of our history with our children. Point out that when our ancestors came—as pioneers or settlers—they often benefited from broken treaties and banishment of the native people. Christian Peacemaker Teams is involved with a number of indigenous groups in Canada and the U.S. who are struggling for recognition of treaties and other rights.[23]

An exception to the story of free immigration is the sordid history of slavery that brought the ancestors of most African-Americans to these shores. We will never know the full effect of their inhuman treatment for 300 years. But we do know that several decades of civil rights laws and affirmative action have not gone far enough in healing those wounds.

Older people and people with disabilities are also often treated as if on the margins of society. Have books and magazines in your home with various people and various cultures. The more your children see of the world's variety of people portrayed positively in their homes, the more they will be able to feel at home in their world.[24]

16. Build bridges with other people.

There are many ways to broaden your understandings and connections locally. Go to stores, restaurants, and diversity events where you will learn about other cultures. Encourage your children to invite friends over from different backgrounds than your own. Visit congregations that include people of other cultural or denominational backgrounds. Attend a community Thanksgiving service. Sing in an interracial choir. Join others at prayer vigils marking tragic events. As a family, Sunday school class, or small group at church, link with a similar group from a congregation with members from another culture. Continuing friendships can rarely be planned and are always a gift. Reaching across cultures is even trickier, but there is even less chance of a connection happening if you don't leave your comfort zone.

17. Explore alternative views of history.

School history texts don't do justice to the bitter experiences of native tribes of North America, African-Americans, new immigrants, and people from particular backgrounds during wars (for example, the U.S. internment camps for Japanese during World War II). Businesses have encouraged people to come to the U.S. to work without giving them basic benefits of residents in exchange (for instance, the Chinese who built railroads in the 1800s and modern Mexican migrant farm workers).[25]

We must own up to the ways our nations have treated people unjustly. Learn about the native peoples who inhabited your hometown area and what became of them. Learn the history of African-Americans, whose unpaid labor created much wealth in the U.S.

Books provide biographies and historical accounts of many people of color and women whose stories are underrepresented in most school curricula. They can also introduce ways of seeing history other than recounting wars, major world powers, and political leaders.[26]

18. Discuss white privilege and anti-racism.

Address issues of white privilege with your children. This isn't hard after talking about the way people who are different (native peoples, African-Americans, Irish, etc.) have been treated. Discuss the institutional power that distinguishes individual prejudice and actions from systemic racism. Point out situations where these have been evident in your experiences and in societal and church institutions. (If you have a problem coming up with examples, contact anyone you know who is not European-American.) Not taking a stand fails to challenge lingering racism in society, so discuss ways your family can be openly anti-racist. The more your children see you interacting with sensitivity and being inclusive, the more they will be able to respect their world's diversity.[27] People of color need to address internalized oppression.[28]

19. Connect Jesus' actions toward marginalized people with ours today.

The Pharisees' disdain for poor and sick people, foreigners, and women is echoed in the second-class status given immigrants, poor, old, sick people, and women in today's society. How do we value those whom society doesn't treat with value? Nursing home residents, particularly those without nearby relatives or friends, are some of the loneliest people around. Many opportunities to volunteer exist there for adults and young teens: wheelchair escorts simply take people to various activities and return them to their rooms.

When one teenager discovered that a man attending her church was homeless, she spent a long time discussing this with her Sunday school teacher who had invited him. She found out that the next Sunday was his birthday and bought him a watch (he rode the bus to the community college and needed to arrive on time), bus tokens, and a gift certificate to his favorite restaurant. She talked this over with her teacher who went with her to give this man the gift. Her teacher said that one of the best things she could do was just to acknowledge him and say hi, since so many people just look the other way. At home, she shared, "I know I can't really do anything about his situation. I can't find him a job and I can't get him a place to live. But I can pray for him."

PLAYING, TOYS, AND GAMES

Parents who see no place for using tanks and guns in real life won't want these as toys for their children. War toys—guns, action figures, video and computer games in a war setting—encourage children to stay fixed on fighting, violence, and even mutilation.[29]

Yet many parents still puzzle over how to respond to war play. "Absolutely anything can turn into a gun in our house," said one exasperated parent, "even a banana!"

Children's play is the work of their early lives, in which they make sense of themselves and their world. Parents walk a fine line between outlawing certain behaviors (perhaps making them even more appealing) and permitting behaviors that may grow more violent with time.

20. Remember that children imitate what they see.

Many toys are spin-offs from TV shows or movies, as are many "scripts" that define children's play. Parents need to be aware of the link between the two. This is addressed further in the next section on television. In their book, *Who's Calling the Shots?: How to Respond Effectively to Children's Fascination with War Play and War Toys*, Nancy Carlsson-Paige and Diane Levin wrote of children's free-time activity:

> Many of the ideas do not come from the children's own minds nor are they expressive of children's needs . . . They come from the television programs and toys, more specifically the people who make and sell them.[30]

These authors also drew from Piaget's work in contrasting play and imitation. To summarize, play is dramatic, constructive, elaborate, and creative (the children's own evolving script), whereas imitation is narrow and repetitive (the marketers' script).

Parents need to be more aware than ever of how their children are playing and be willing to step in with constructive suggestions and pertinent questions.

Part of making sense of their world involves children trying out various responses to life situations. When they focus on violent responses, they severely limit their learning options. Susan Mark Landis, Peace Advocate for the Mennonite Church USA, said, "Perhaps if children are told that solving a play problem violently is not an option, they will learn to seek other options and thus broaden their range of responses. We don't allow our children to 'play' at rape or stealing, why at killing?"

21. Intervene creatively.

Once when my children were playing with neighbors at the park "killing the bad guys" who were terrorizing them, I told them I knew a secret about these particular bad guys: they fell asleep whenever anyone sang a song. For a while, I narrated the sneaky approach of the bad guys, and we kept coming up on the spur of the moment with songs to lull them into sleep.

Carlsson-Paige and Levin suggest offering ideas about new ways to use a toy that is only being used for fighting. "When your child is playing with He-Man, a comment like, 'My, you've used He-Man so much he's gotten really dirty. Maybe you should give him a bath,' can add a new dimension to his play."[31] Talk to children about the situations they are dealing with: "What is that bad guy's name?" "Do you think (the name) has any children?" "What does God do with bad guys?" "What does God do with us when we've done bad things?"

22. Find exciting alternatives for violent games and toys.

For younger children, encourage play scenarios like fighting fires or floods and chasing monsters or dragons. Look for alternative play figures that emphasize "helpful heroes." Give the children shovels, buckets, and small garden tools to excavate in dirt or the sandbox. They might wear hard hats to dig roads or a tunnel. Older children can construct a small boat or clubhouse with lumber scraps.

Children enjoy using flashlights to hunt monsters or to explore the dark basement or closet. (This also involves running and squealing.) In warm weather, squirt animals or dish detergent squeeze bottles can be used to wet a chosen target. Water hoses and swimming suits work together really well. [32]

23. Provide books where good triumphs over evil, without violence as central to the story line.

Besides play, another way to vicariously try out different responses to life situations is through books. In fairy tales and folktales from around the world, main characters overcome great obstacles to reach their goals. The plots are imaginative, and children can see themselves as part of the unfolding drama, without needing to leave the safety of their living room couches. *Tatterhood and Other Tales* is a classic for both boys and girls with tales of magic and adventure that portray active, courageous women and girls as heroines.[33]

Many fairy tales and exciting children and youth books do include a lot of violence, accepting it unquestioningly. C. S. Lewis's Narnian chronicles, Tolkien's *Lord of the Rings* trilogy, Brian Jacques' Redwall series, and the latter Harry Potter books feature violence in overcoming evil. But then, so do many favorite Bible stories: the Flood, the exodus, the taking of the Promised Land, and Samson. It isn't fair to the biblical record to sanitize these stories. So, again, we can talk with our children about the violence in books and in the Bible. We can talk about how God wanted the Israelites to depend on him, and not on their own military might—as in the story of Gideon preparing to go fight, the taking of Jericho, and others.[34] We can talk about Jesus being the closest example to how God wants people to live and how he chose to be killed rather than to kill.

24. Challenge traditional gender expectations.

Sam, a kindergartner, told his mom he wanted his hair cut so it wouldn't look like a girl's hair. His three-year-old brother Jacob piped up, "I'd like *my* hair to look like a girl's hair!" (Jacob also still allowed my daughter to put barrettes in his hair and paint his fingernails.)

When they reach school, most children quickly become sensitive to gender identity. Carlsson-Paige and Levin write, "Today's toy and play culture is more gender-specific than ever . . . before, play was more flexible, kids could find more room for common ground."[35]

After seeing and falling in love with Disney's princesses, our daughter Jazzmin's play scripts became rather disturbing. She instructed a boy playmate to carry her coat for her and then ask her if she was cold. Helplessness, dependence, and a demure spirit seemed to go along with the feminine object of affection in many fairy tales and cartoon videos.

One option is to try to keep Barbie dolls and Disney movies that idolize women away from young children, at least in your own home. Snow White and Sleeping Beauty are both saved from a lifeless state by the prince hero. These are too often the dominant female images in the movies—girls living for the day they get married.[36] Cartoon females, as well as Barbie-type dolls, have out-of-this-world body proportions, hair, and complexions. A friend relates her experience:

> Rosie's babysitter gave her a Barbie doll—her first; we hadn't wanted her to have one. She was probably three at the time. I was trying to minimize the effect on her. I said, "She looks weird to me. Her legs and neck are way too long and her waist is way too small." Rosie said, "You shouldn't make fun of her for how she looks, Mama. That's just how long her legs are."

Another option is to provide plenty of alternative toys, stories, and movies alongside. There are many books about strong, independent, and smart girls. There are even princess stories with strong princesses. Find books for your sons about sensitive, nurturing boys. Share these with your children.[37]

Discuss how women you know have used their skills in life. Talk about what men and women in nontraditional careers do during the day. Support people who nurture their families but whose lifestyles go against the traditional or societal grain.

Since children's play usually evolves from scenes they've seen, modeling non-stereotypical roles may be the most effective encouragement parents can give for flexible play. Jim and Kathleen McGinnis find strong role models for children in:

> a father who expresses his emotions openly, hugs and kisses his children, listens to his children's feelings, takes care of infant needs, works in the kitchen, is interested in poetry or music or art . . . [and] a mother who pursues her own path of intellectual development, expresses her own opinions, does not depend on

a man to hammer a nail or pump gas for her, participates in sports according to her own interests.[38]

TELEVISION, MOVIES, AND VIDEOS

The statistics are sobering. Television viewing correlates with poor academic performance, more sedentary lifestyles, obesity in children, and less interactive family times. Add to this the effects of repeatedly viewing violent actions.

Today the data linking violence in the media to violence in society are stronger than those linking cancer and tobacco. Ninety-nine percent of more than 3,500 studies on the effects of media violence have shown a correlation between watching violence on TV and committing acts of real-life violence.[39]

> The most benign product you are going to get from the networks are twenty-two-minute sitcoms or cartoons providing instant solutions for all of life's problems, interlaced with commercials telling you what a slug you are if you don't ingest the right sugary substances and don't wear the right shoes.
>
> The worst product your child is going to get from the networks is represented by one TV commentator who told me, "Well, we only have one really violent show on our network, and that is NYPD Blue. I'll admit that that is bad, but it is only one night a week." I wondered at the time how she would feel if someone said, "Well, I only beat my wife in front of the kids one night a week."[40]

In addition to increasing acts of violence, the sexual references-per-hour during prime time television were three times higher in 1999 than in 1989.[41] Deborah Roffman, educator and author in the area of sex education, said, "Sex is portrayed on television and in movies as dehumanizing and demeaning—the meaning is literally taken out. The message again and again is sex is recreation."[42]

Media executives and advertisers know that our emotions focus our attention, aid our memory, and motivate our behavior. They talk about the "jps factor" (jolts per show). TV shows and video games are geared more toward jolts than toward reflection or clear thinking.[43] I too can attest to this jolt-factor. When my five-year-old changed channels from the PBS show she was watching, we were both mesmerized by the fast-paced, high-impact nature of both the show and the ad that came on. Children need parents who set limits on what to watch, and, when watching with children are willing to say, "Let's talk about what we just saw and what it means."

25. Pay attention to shows your child watches and games your child plays on the screen.

Limiting the time your children spend viewing violent and sexist TV images may be one of the most important steps you can take in teaching peace. Time watching videos and playing computer games raises some of the same issues as TV watching, and the number of hours spent there is rising.[44] Each family needs to set screen time guidelines and revisit them from time to time. The American Academy of Pediatrics (AAP) recommends no more than 1 to 2 hours of quality TV and videos a day for older children and none for children under the age of 2.[45]

In an average U.S. home, the TV was on 7 hours and 40 minutes a day in 2000. Children ages 2 to 17 watched TV almost 20 hours a week, with all citizens averaging 26 hours a week in 1998.[46] More than 10 hours per week of TV viewing has been shown to negatively affect academic achievement.[47] U.S. children view 20,000 TV commercials a year.[48] The average child in the U.S. views 200,000 violent acts on TV by age 18.[49]

In Canada, children watched about 16 hours a week of TV in 1999, with the average Canadian watching 22 hours in 1998. This amount decreased since 1986, although attendance at movie theaters rose steadily from 1992 to 1999. In 1998, teens spent an average of 5 hours a week playing video games and Canadians spent more and more time online (surpassing U.S. figures).[50]

Decide how many hours of screen time are allowed each day or week. What videos, shows, and movies are off-limits? Visit the National Institute on Media and the Family's website for movie, TV show ratings, and computer game recommendations. [51]

When you choose to watch videos, watch them with your children when possible and talk about what you are seeing. The AAP suggests asking children to think about what would happen if the same type of violent act were committed in real life as on the screen. Would anyone die or go to jail? Would anyone be sad? Would the violence solve problems or create them?[52]

26. Help sponsor a TV-Turnoff Week at your church or school.

The TV-Turnoff Network has many facts on TV viewing and ideas to help your family curb TV use. (See their box above.)[53] Work with the PTA or church education committee to sponsor a TV-Turnoff Week. Include a family activity night with a music group, storyteller, or square dance. Give incentives for children to go the whole week without TV—incentives like coupons for pizza, or books donated by local businesses.

FAMILY PLEDGE OF NONVIOLENCE

This simple statement is one way to share with your children the interconnected issues presented in this book as a shalom lifestyle.[54]

27. Ask your children to help rate your family.

Before taking the pledge (or periodically after taking it), invite family members to assess your family's strengths and weaknesses in the various pledge areas. This simple exercise, available on the companion website (http://peace.mennolink.org/teachpeace) can help start a discussion about specific ways your family might become more peaceful.

28. Take the Family Pledge of Nonviolence.

The inexpensive booklet, *Families Creating Circles of Peace: A Guide for Living the Pledge of Nonviolence*, gives helpful ideas for taking the pledge as a family. It also includes stories, suggestions, activities, and other resources to help people live out the pledge in daily life. *Kids Creating Circles of Peace* is a companion resource. (An alternative is for your family to write your own pledge.)[55]

Discussion questions

1. Which of these suggestions for a shalom lifestyle have you implemented in your family? Share your experience with the group. Which suggestions would you like to try? Why?
2. How have you meaningfully incorporated worship into your family life?
3. What have you done as a family to live out your peace beliefs by way of sharing physically with others or advocating on others' behalf?
4. Do you and your children spend time with people from other ethnic backgrounds? If not, what might you do to take this step?
5. What aspects of your children's play make you uncomfortable? Do you have guidelines about watching TV and videos? About playing computer games? If you do, are they working for your family?
6. It can be hard when other children talk about TV shows or movies that are off-limits in your family, or when other children have more stuff. What are ways to help children feel confident and okay with your choices?

Family Pledge of Nonviolence

Making peace must start within ourselves and in our family. Each of us, members of the _____family, commit ourselves as best we can to become nonviolent and peaceable people.

To Respect Self and Others
To respect myself, to affirm others and to avoid uncaring criticism,
hateful words, physical attacks and self-destructive behavior.

To Communicate Better
To share my feelings honestly, to look for safe ways to express my anger,
and to work at solving problems peacefully.

To Listen
To listen carefully to one another, especially those who disagree with me,
and to consider others' feelings and needs rather than insist on having my own way.

To Forgive
To apologize and make amends when I have hurt another,
to forgive others, and to keep from holding grudges.

To Respect Nature
To treat the environment and all living things,
including our pets, with respect and care.

To Play Creatively
To select entertainment and toys that support our family's values and to
avoid entertainment that makes violence look exciting, funny or acceptable.

To Be Courageous
To challenge violence in all its forms whenever I encounter it, whether at home,
at school, at work, or in the community, and to stand with others
who are treated unfairly.

This is our pledge. These are our goals. We will check ourselves on what we have pledged once a month on _____ for the next twelve months so that we can help each other become more peaceable people.

Pledging family members sign below:

_____   _____

_____   _____

_____   _____

"Eliminating violence, one family at a time, starting with our own."

Families Against Violence Advocacy Network • c/o Institute for Peace and Justice Network
4144 Lindell Blvd. #408 • St. Louis, MO 63108 • (314) 533-4445 • Fax: (314) 715-6455
Email: ipj@ipj-ppj.org • Website: www.ipj-ppj.org

Chapter 5

Shalom Living: The Global Village

> When indeed shall we learn that we are
> all related one to the other, that we are
> all members of one body?
>
> —Helen Keller[1]

There is so much to learn from paying attention to the world around us. And when there are so many unjust and *unpeaceful* situations in our world, we will naturally address these with our children. Focus on one country or region of the world, and take action—write letters and send health or school kits. Keep a globe handy so you can locate these places. Or put a map on the wall and put photos of church workers near where they live.[2]

1. Build bridges with other people in the world.

There are various ways to connect your child and family to people in other countries. One tangible way is to put together health or school kits for a relief organization like Mennonite Central Committee (MCC). Your family could sponsor a family or school in need of financial resources through MCC's Global Family Program of sponsorship and education. (Beware of sponsorship programs with high overhead costs—ask to see their financial statement.) Sponsoring an exchange student or MCC International Visitor Exchange Program (IVEP) participant is another way to become involved in the life of someone from another country.[3] Another idea for your child to consider is a pen pal or e-pal. (See box.)

Keep in touch with people from your church who go into international service. The continued contact benefits them while providing your children with information about how people around the world live and how your country's policies help or hurt. Or, contact a mission or service agency where your family can be paired with one of the agency's families in another country.

Emphasize that the life of everyone on the planet is equally valuable in God's eyes. Children will not get this from society when the news they see focuses narrowly on national or local issues. Here again, we can provide them with magazines and books that portray God's global family.[4] The more your children know people in other countries, the more they will question foreign policy that labels whole countries as evil and military actions that cost civilian lives.

Growing up, I had a pen pal from Japan. Through Mayumi I learned interesting things about Japanese society and educational system.[6] Another avenue for relating today is the Internet, which enables e-pal connections for your children or family. John D. Smucker, a high school teacher in Indiana, explored the idea with international service workers. In November of 2001, he linked thirty-five juniors and seniors with e-pals in Nazareth who were close to their age. John said, "I have found that the best place to start to find connections is through your home congregations . . . Prayer takes on a more global outlook and students can scrutinize the news our media feeds us about other countries more closely because it may not be consistent with what their e-pals are telling them."

2. Advocate on behalf of others in the world.

Amnesty International (AI) focuses on human rights abuses worldwide. They have various letter-writing programs on behalf of individuals. Families with younger children could easily participate in their annual Holiday Card Action. Their AIKids page on the web also has a children's edition of Urgent Actions, and various educational activities.[5]

In 1999, my eight-year-old daughter helped her uncle package a weekly ration for an Iraqi family. They sent it to a congressman to protest ten years of war, sanctions, and bombing against the Iraqi people. Her letter read,

Dear Mr. Spratt,

This is not enough food for a week! My family would eat this in less than a day. Please lift the sanctions.

3. Teach your children creation care.

The earth cannot sustain everyone living at the level of those of us in North America. One calculation gives 1.7 hectares (3.9 acres) of biologically productive area available per capita. In 1997, U.S. citizens used 10.3 hectares per person and Canadians 7.7. We are essentially overusing our natural capital to finance current consumption.[7] Reducing consumption and living on less money, however, aren't always necessarily connected. Recycling and buying locally may not save many dollars, but they use fewer resources. And none of these lifestyle issues have anything simple about them, despite what the term simple living might suggest. Those of us in North America, however, do need a wake-up call; we need to begin seriously addressing what standard of living reflects justice in our world today, and how to move in that direction.[8]

> *Treat the earth well. It was not given to you by your parents. It was lent to you by your children.*
>
> —Kenyan proverb

4. Talk about war.

Children may wonder why people start and fight wars. What makes people do such horrible things? One simple

March 2002

Dear President Bush,

Please don't do war in *any* country because that's not okay. It hurts people and it's never okay to kill people.

Jazzmin

analogy (for the attack on September 11, 2001, for example) is a child who has felt picked on time after time. Suddenly that child may do something nasty in return. The action seems to be out of the blue—but it isn't. Understanding the history doesn't make the nasty act okay, but it does make it more comprehensible.

Those of us engaged in peacemaking need to be especially careful not to demonize people in the military. "Christians tend to get very angry toward others who sin differently than they do," commented the director of an organization ministering to people with AIDS.[9] Part of peacemaking is being able to see from another's point of view and, even when that person's view is entirely opposed to our own, to figure out how to love them. This is God's example for us in Jesus.

Part of teaching peace to our children is sharing with them the rationale behind different perspectives and helping them share their own respectfully with others. A friend relates:

> Our daughter, who attends a Catholic high school, found the school's response to the September 11 attacks and the subsequent bombing disturbing. She began to realize more clearly that peace is important to her and that not all Christians view war and peace like we do. One night her English assignment was to write a letter of support to a serviceman. After considering a number of options, she chose to write a letter to a member of Christian Peacemaker Teams expressing support for the work of CPT. She also wrote a cover letter to her teacher explaining that she could not do the assignment because she did not support our country's military involvement in Afghanistan.

Sami and the Time of the Troubles by Florence Parry Heide does a good job of explaining aspects of living during a war to elementary children.[10] Find Lebanon on a map, as well as Israel/Palestine and other areas in the news. Sami is a ten-year-old boy in Beirut who has lived with war all his life, as have children in other countries you might mention. Living in a basement with his family, he has a growing desire to work for peace and finds ways to do so.

5. Acknowledge questions without answers.

God doesn't expect parents to have answers to all questions about evil, pacifism, Hitler, or terrorists. And, fortunately, God did not put us in charge of keeping the peace in a world full of people who have rejected God's sovereignty. (It's hard enough to do the things that God *has* told us to do, without taking on additional tasks!) We are told:

> You shall love the Lord your God with all your heart, and with all your soul, and with all your might. Keep these words that I am commanding you today in your heart. Recite them to your children and talk about them when you are at home and when you are away, when you lie down and when you rise.[11]

Jesus reiterated this in the New Testament. When asked which was the first commandment, he mentioned *both* the passage from Deuteronomy and one from Leviticus 19:18 when he added:

> The second is this, "You shall love your neighbor as yourself." There is no other commandment greater than these.[12]

Discussion questions:

1. Do your children know people who live in other parts of the world?
2. How do you talk about wars going on and the role of the U.S. in them? What alternate news sources do you use?

Chapter 6

Working Together:
The Church and the Home

> *If you head into unfamiliar woods, you had better find companions first; if you want to buck traffic, organize a convoy. To nonconform freely we must strengthen each other.*
>
> —Doris Janzen Longacre [1]

1. Use curricula that integrates peacemaking.

As a congregation, choose a curriculum for children and youth that integrates peacemaking stories and Scriptures. Check the Mennonite Publishing Network website to see what Sunday school and Bible school curriculum materials are available: www.mph.org/cp/.

2. Host a Peace Reader Program.

Two people can easily coordinate a Peace Reader Program for your congregation or even several local congregations. The program may run over the summer months, or during the winter (when there are not competing library programs).

You can download forms from the companion website (http://peace.mennolink.org/teachpeace). Find a suitable reward to give to participants—for example, persuade a local ice cream shop or café to donate Ben and Jerry's Peace Pop ice cream bars. Determine points for different appropriate activities and alter the guidelines sheet accordingly. Make coupons to give to those who have earned a reward. Consider including adults in the program (who read books on their own or to children).

When the program is done, host an open house or reception. Display posters children drew, and invite singers and instrumentalists to perform favorite peace songs. Read a few of the favorite books aloud. *The Butter Battle Book* and *Rumpelstiltskin's Daughter* are possibilities.[2]

3. Hold a draft preparation event.

It's ironic that churches often don't teach against participation in war when no war is going on. Then when military action begins, they discover it's too late. Hold regular events for members to consider their own faithful responses if there were war, and review stories of pacifists during previous wars; this prepares the congregation for peaceful action. One responsibility of a congregation is to create experiences for youth that help them solidify their peacemaking views.

For either of the following activities, it would help if the Sunday school class spent several weeks or months beforehand looking at historical and biblical information about conscientious objection to the draft, as well as Christians who have participated in military service. Part of this study can include questions for parents to address with their children at home.[3]

Fill out forms documenting beliefs for nonparticipation, or participation, in armed conflict. Obtain peacemaker registration packets from Mennonite Central Committee.[4] Ask each person from a certain age up to fill out one of the forms, including supporting evidence: Scripture and life experiences that have helped form their views. If people believe they could participate in the military in some form, have them justify those convictions. In subsequent years, they can update these forms, using the help of parents, teachers, or mentors if needed. Youth from fifteen to twenty-six should keep these on file; medical professionals should keep them up to age forty-five.

Start a biannual event for high school students. Begin the evening with a video like *The Good War and Those Who Refused to Fight It* or *Change of Command.*[5] Ahead of time, ask several adults to form a mock draft board. Distribute numbers to all high school students present and draw or choose from those numbers one at a time. Ask each student one or two questions about their willingness or unwillingness to take part in military action. Make them give reasons and supporting information. Or, hold the event for the whole congregation. Give numbers to all willing to participate as they enter. Offer a mentor to help out youth who might want one (the goal is to strengthen convictions and not embarrass youth).

4. Go in peace.

May we, as families in partnership with our congregations, model radical faithfulness to the God who calls us to be peacemakers in our world.

> *God, each day may my faith generate shalom:*
> *Let my dreams image shalom,*
> *Let my mind think shalom,*
> *Let my heart ignite shalom,*
> *Let my words invite shalom,*
> *Let my deeds reflect shalom,*
> *God, may your shalom transform my soul.*

—Atlee Beechy[6]

Notes

Introduction

1. Kathleen and James McGinnis, *Parenting for Peace and Justice: Ten Years Later* (New York: Orbis Books, 1990).
2. Nancy Lee Cecil with Patricia L. Roberts, *Raising Peaceful Children in a Violent World* (San Diego: LuraMedia, 1995).
3. The world income gap between the richest 20 percent and poorest 20 percent increased from 30 to 1 in 1960 to 74 to 1 in 1997. (*MCC Washington Office Guide to Economic Globalization*, December 2001).

Chapter 1

1. Perry B. Yoder, *Shalom: The Bible's Word for Salvation, Justice, and Peace* (Newton, Kan.: Faith & Life Press, 1987), 22.
2. In John's Gospel, Jesus uses a whip to drive sheep and cattle from the temple. The interpretation that Jesus also used the whip on people (the money changers and merchants) is challenged by theologians such as John Howard Yoder, in *The Politics of Jesus* (Grand Rapids, Eerdmans, 1995), 41-43.
3. For a helpful explanation of Matthew 5:38-42, an often misinterpreted text, see Walter Wink, *Engaging the Powers: Discernment and Resistance in a World of Domination* (Minneapolis: Fortress Press, 1992), 175-89.
4. Yoder, *Shalom*, 19-20.
5. For an in-depth look at some of these issues, see Ronald J. Sider, *Completely Pro-Life: Building a Consistent Stance on Abortion, the Family, Nuclear Weapons, the Poor* (Downers Grove, Ill.: InterVarsity Press, 1987).
6. National Conference of Catholic Bishops, *The Challenge of Peace: God's Promise and Our Response* (Boston: St. Paul's Editions, 1983), 88-89.

Chapter 2

1. Mary Joan Park, *Peacemaking for Little Friends: Tips, Lessons and Resources for Parents and Teachers* (St. Paul: Little Friends for Peace, 1985), dedication page.
2. Robert Coles, *The Moral Intelligence of Children: How to Raise a Moral Child* (New York: Penguin, 1998), 169-70.
3. Lynn Okagaki, K. Hammond, and L. Seamon, "Socialization of Religious Beliefs," *Journal of Applied Developmental Psychology* 20 (1999): 273-94.
4. Katherine Scholes, *Peace Begins with You* (San Francisco: Sierra Club, 1990). Nancy Lee Cecil with Patricia L. Roberts, *Raising Peaceful Children in a Violent World* (San Diego: LuraMedia, 1995).
5. For a powerful look at God's grace, see Philip Yancey, *What's So Amazing About Grace?* (Grand Rapids, Mich.: Zondervan, 1997).
6. Doris Janzen Longacre et al., *Living More with Less* (Scottdale, Pa.: Herald Press, 1980), 17.

Chapter 3

1. *Confession of Faith in a Mennonite Perspective* (Scottdale, Pa.: Herald Press, 1995), 12.
2. Ephesians 4:24 and 5:1, Matthew 5.
3. Becky Bailey, *Easy to Love, Difficult to Discipline: The Seven Basic Skills for Turning Conflict into Cooperation* (New York: William Morrow, 2000), 2.
4. Jerry Camery-Hoggatt, *Grapevine: The Spirituality of Gossip* (Scottdale, Pa.: Herald Press, 2001) speaks directly to this issue.
5. For a fantastic, easy-to-read manual with practical help on dialogue, anger, decision making, and more marital issues, see Susan Heitler, *The Power of Two: Secrets to a Stronger and Loving Marriage* (Oakland, Calif.: New Harbinger Publications, 1997).

6. Jane Nelsen, *Positive Discipline,* 2d ed. (New York: Ballantine, 1996) and Jane Nelsen, Lynn Lott, and H. Stephen Glenn, *Positive Discipline A-Z: 1001 Solutions for Everyday Parenting Problems,* 2d ed. (Rocklin, Calif.: Prima, 1999).

7. Burt Berlowe, Elizabeth Lonning, and Joseph Cress, *The Peaceful Parenting Handbook* (San Jose, Calif.: Resource Publications, 2001). Nancy Lee Cecil with Patricia L. Roberts, *Raising Peaceful Children in a Violent World* (San Diego: LuraMedia, 1995).

8. James Dobson, "Anger Most Common Error in Discipline," *The Goshen News* (14 April 2002): A4.

9. Astrid Lindgren in Jim McGinnis et al., *Families Creating a Circle of Peace: A Guide for Living the Family Pledge of Nonviolence* (St. Louis: Families Against Violence Advocacy Network, 1996), 26.

10. Ephesians 4:26.

11. Matthew 23:13-33; Mark 11:15-17; John 18:19-23.

12. Dorothea Lachner, *Andrew's Angry Words* (New York: North-South Books,1997) is a favorite that follows a trail of misplaced angry words.

13. Susan Canizares's multiethnic *Feelings* (New York: Scholastic,1999) includes ways to talk with very young children. Norma Simon, *I Was So Mad!* (Morton Grove, Ill.: Albert Whitman, 1991) is a classic from 1974, still in print. Betsy Everitt, *Mean Soup* (San Diego: Harcourt Brace, 1995) features Horace and his creative mom. For 8-12 year olds, see Jerry Wilde, *Hot Stuff to Help Kids Chill Out: The Anger Management Book* (Richmond, Ind.: LGR Publishing, 1997). Parenting Press has some excellent books, most by Elizabeth Crary, in four different series for children ranging from ages 4 to 11. They deal with emotions and situations of conflict, allowing the child to choose from different responses, exploring vicariously what might happen. See page 70 for Parenting Press website.

14. Different self-tests titled "Conflict: How Do YOUth Respond?" in versions for grades 3-5, 6-8, 9-12, and one for adults may be downloaded from the companion website (http://peace.mennolink.org/teachpeace). Instructions for scoring and interpreting scores are included, along with a one-hour format for using this resource with groups of children. Families, Sunday school classes, and youth groups might find this activity helpful.

15. Fran Schmidt and Alice Friedman, *Creative Conflict Solving for Kids* (Miami: Grace Contrino Abrams Peace Education Foundation, 1991).

16. Kathleen McGinnis and Barbara Oehlberg, S*tarting Out Right: Nurturing Young Children as Peacemakers* (Bloomington, Ind.: Meyer Stone Books, 1988).

17. For more in-depth, practical information regarding sibling conflicts, see Elaine Mazlish and Adele Faber's *Siblings Without Rivalry: How to Help Your Children Live Together So You Can Live Too* (New York: William Morrow, 1998).

18. Recommended titles for more help: Mary Sheedy Kurcinka, *Raising Your Spirited Child* (New York: Harper Perennial, 1992) and *Raising Your Spirited Child Workbook* (New York: HarperCollins, 1998). To help sort out behavioral and chemical issues and for a better understanding of various temperamental issues involved with hard-to-raise children and helpful responses: Stanley Turecki, *The Difficult Child,* rev. ed. (New York: Bantam, 1989). Ross W. Greene, *The Explosive Child,* 2d ed. (New York: HarperCollins, 2001) has more in-depth background and suggestions for parents of "inflexible and explosive" children.

19. Derek Glover and Netta Cartwright, *Towards Bully Free Schools: Interventions in Action* (Buckingham, England: Open University Press, 1997). Rachel Simmons, *Odd Girl Out: The Hidden Culture of Aggression in Girls* (New York: Harcourt Brace, 2002). Several other books provide helpful tools for your children when faced with a bullying kind of neighborhood or schoolyard situation. Judith Vigna's classic *Anyhow, I'm Glad I Tried* (Morton Grove, Ill.: Albert Whitman: 1978), is a realistic tale about a girl whose efforts at peacemaking seem futile. Phyllis Reynolds Naylor, *The King of the Playground* (New York: Simon & Schuster, 1994) and Dan Millman and T. Taylor Bruce's *Secret of the Peaceful Warrior: A Story About Courage and Love* (Tiburon, Calif.: H. J. Kramer, 1991) give children new ways to view threats and strength. Carl W. Bosch, *Bully on the Bus* (Seattle: Parenting Press, 1988), a choose-your-own-ending story for older children, lets them explore the consequences of the different possible responses to bullying.

Chapter 4

1. Robert McAfee Brown, *Making Peace in a Global Village* (Philadelphia: Westminster, 1981), 15.
2. Wayne Muller, "Whatever Happened to Sunday?" *U.S.A. Weekend* (4 April 1999): 4. See also his *Sabbath: Restoring the Sacred Rhythm of Rest* (New York: Random House, 1999). Another excellent book is Marva Dawn, *Keeping the Sabbath Wholly: Ceasing, Resting, Embracing, Feasting* (Grand Rapids: Eerdmans, 1989).
3. Jeanne Zimmerly Jantzi, *Parent Trek: Nurturing Creativity and Care in Our Children* (Scottdale, Pa.: Herald Press, 2001). Marcia Kelly et al., *One Hundred Graces: Mealtime Blessings* (New York: Random House, 1997).
4. A Peters projection map more accurately shows the area of different countries than the standard Mercator projection.
5. Elizabeth Crary, *Pick Up Your Socks . . . And Other Skills Growing Children Need!: A Practical Guide to Raising Responsible Children* (Seattle: Parenting Press, 1990) has a chapter on "Household Jobs and Responsibilities," with a chart that gives age ranges for when children can manage different tasks. Jane Nelsen, *Positive Discipline*, 2d ed. (New York: Ballantine, 1996) has a section, "Chores, Age Appropriate" that lists different chores from ages 2 to 12.
6. Kathleen and James McGinnis, *Parenting for Peace and Justice: Ten Years Later* (New York: Orbis Books, 1990), 35-9. Also see Nancy Lee Cecil with Patricia L. Roberts, *Raising Peaceful Children in a Violent World* (San Diego, Calif.: LuraMedia, 1995), 59-70, on Family Peace Meetings that blend the peace table idea with a family meeting. Jane Nelsen, Lynn Lott, and H. Stephen Glenn, *Positive Discipline A-Z: 1001 Solutions for Everyday Parenting Problems*, 2d ed. (Rocklin, Calif.: Prima, 1999) has a brief but helpful discussion of family meetings. More detailed information is included in Nelsen, *Positive Discipline*, chapter 8.
7. Jim McGinnis et al., *Families Creating a Circle of Peace: A Guide for Living the Family Pledge of Nonviolence* (St. Louis: Families Against Violence Advocacy Network, 1996), 7.
8. Matthew 25: 40, 45.
9. *MCC Washington Office Guide to Economic Globalization* (December 2001).
10. For more on biblical economics, see Donald B. Kraybill, *The Upside-Down Kingdom*, rev. ed. (Scottdale, Pa.: Herald Press, 2003), chapters 5 and 6. For more on Christianity and wealth, see Ronald J. Sider, *Rich Christians in an Age of Hunger: Moving from Affluence to Generosity*, 4th ed. (Dallas: Word Publishing, 1997).
11. If your children chafe at the difference in your standard of living and lifestyle choices compared to others, read Byrd Baylor, *The Table Where Rich People Sit* (New York: Atheneum, 1994).
12. Peter Menzel and Charles Mann, *Material World: A Global Family Portrait* (San Francisco: Sierra Club, 1994). David Schrock-Shenk ed., *Basic Trek: Venture into a World of Enough, the Original 28-Day Journey* (Scottdale, Pa.: Herald Press, 2002) is a good resource for group (or personal) study. It looks at family living and how much is enough from various perspectives. Murray Sheard, *Living Simply: Studies in Learning to Live as Jesus Did* (Auckland: World Vision of New Zealand, 1999) can also serve as a relevant group study. (Available from Alternatives: see page 69. Jeanne Zimmerly Jantzi's *Parent Trek* has ideas for sharing this journey with your children.
13. Barbara DeGrote Sorensen in *Break Forth into Joy! Beyond a Consumer Lifestyle*, prod. Burst Video Film, Inc. (Alternatives for Simple Living, 1995). This video examines our search for fulfillment through material possessions, sharing people's feelings, thoughts, and practical ideas. The full transcript is available on the web (www.simpleliving.org/Archives/VideoScripts/BreakforthJoy.html).
14. Ronald J. Sider, *Rich Christians in an Age of Hunger: A Biblical Study* (New York: Paulist Press, 1977), 175-78.
15. *Federal Register* 67 (14 February 2002): 6931-33. For up-to-date figures, see the U.S. Dept. of Health and Human Services website: http://aspe.hhs.gov/poverty/. Unfortunately, official poverty figures (used to calculate public assistance) don't reflect even most basic living costs. See the discussion about Basic Family Budgets by the Economic Policy Institute: www.epinet.org.
16. To calculate these figures in future years, see "What Is a Dollar Worth?" from the Federal Reserve Bank of Minneapolis: http://woodrow.mpls.srb.fed.us/research/data/us/calc/

17. Jo Robinson and Jean Coppock Staeheli, *Unplug the Christmas Machine*, rev. ed. (New York: William Morrow, 1991) is a good resource from Alternatives. Two others by Alternatives are *Treasury of Celebrations: Create Celebrations That Reflect Your Values and Don't Cost the Earth* (Canada: Northstone, 1997) and *To Celebrate: Reshaping Holidays and Rites of Passage* (Sioux City, Iowa: Alternatives, 1988). See also the chapters on celebrations in Zimmerly Jantzi, *Parent Trek* and Doris Janzen Longacre, *Living More with Less* (Scottdale, Pa.: Herald Press, 1980). A new Canadian initiative is Buy Nothing Christmas (see page 69).

18. Zimmerly Jantzi, *Parent Trek*, 151.

19. Mennonite Central Committee (MCC): see page 70 for contact information. Habitat for Humanity: 800-HABITAT, www.habitat.org (you can find a local affiliate here). The Heifer Project: www.heifer.org.

20. For other good ideas: Alternatives, *Treasury of Celebrations* and *To Celebrate*. Zimmerly Jantzi, *Parent Trek*. Ellen Berry, *Gifts That Make a Difference: How to Buy Hundreds of Great Gifts Sold Through Nonprofits* (Orlando, Fla.: Foxglove, 1992).

21. Mennonite Disaster Service (binational): 717-859-2210. Red Cross: http://redcross.volunteermatch.org/. Habitat for Humanity: 800-HABITAT, www.habitat.org (you can find a local affiliate here).

22. For MCC resources or a catalog see page 70 for contact information. AFSCs catalog can be reached at 215-241-7000 or www.afsc.org. For action alerts and legislative information contact the MCC Washington Office at 202-544-6554 or the MCC Canada Ottawa office at 613-238-7224. The FCNL, U.S. is on the web at www.fcnl.org. Their Legislative Action Center has timely action alerts with contact information, including a daily spot on Congress Today.

23. See CPTs website, www.prairienet.org/cpt, for more information about their efforts.

24. Louise Derman-Sparks, *Anti-Bias Curriculum: Tools for Empowering Young Children* (Washington D.C.: National Association for Education of the Young Child, 1989) has excellent specific strategies for 3-5 year olds and resource lists—including a list of books featuring characters with disabilities. An abundance of excellent multicultural literature has been published in the last decade. Check the companion website (http://peace.mennolink.org/teachpeace) for the Annotated Peace Resource List under "Our Many Cultures" and links to other lists.

25. Eve Bunting, *So Far from the Sea* (New York: Clarion Books, 1998) relates the story of Laura Iwasaki's grandfather, who was assigned to a camp with his Japanese-American family. Jane Thomas, *Lights on the River* (New York: Hyperion, 1994) shares young Teresa's memories of family times in Mexico and visions of daily life as migrant farm workers. Both are excellent picture books for 4-8 year olds. A good book for all ages on native people is Maggie Steincrohn Davis, *Roots of Peace, Seeds of Hope: A Journey for Peacemakers* (Blue Hill, Maine: Heartsong Books, 1994).

26. Betsy Hearne, *Seven Brave Women* (New York: Greenwillow, 1997), is a striking narrative of the author's female ancestors, beginning with her great-great-great-grandmother, who "did great things"—living during a war, but not fighting in it. The colorful picture book continues by generation down to her daughter. A one-of-a-kind nonfiction work is Penny Colman, *Girls: A History of Growing Up Female in America* (New York: Scholastic, 2000). Your older children might enjoy reading James W. Loewen, *Lies My Teacher Told Me: Everything Your American History Textbook Got Wrong* (New York: Touchstone, 1996) and Howard Zinn, *A People's History of the United States: 1492–Present* (New York: HarperCollins, 1999) for corrections to standard histories. James C. Juhnke and Carol Hunter, *The Missing Peace: The Search for Nonviolent Alternatives in United States History* (Waterloo: Pandora Press, 2001) shares little-known facts of nonviolent actions and movements in U.S. history. An Aboriginal book list for children and other educational resources are available by e-mailing: learningcircle@inac.gc.ca

27. Barbara Mathias and Mary Ann French, *40 Ways to Raise a Nonracist Child* (New York: Harper Collins, 1996) is an excellent book co-authored by an African-American and a European-American. Darlene Powell and Derek S. Hopson, *Raising the Rainbow Generation: Teaching Your Children to Be Successful in a Multicultural Society* (New York: Simon & Schuster, 1993) is also good. See *Parenting for Peace and Justice Newsletter* 61 (February 1994), "Building Diversity with Dignity," especially the suggestions on page 7 for members of privileged groups.

28. For an introduction, see Jody Miller Shearer, *Enter the River: Healing Steps from White Privilege Toward Racial Reconciliation* (Scottdale, Pa.: Herald Press, 1994), chapter 5, "How Does Racism Afflict People of Color?" See also Iris de Leon-Hartshorn, Tobin Miller Shearer, and Regina Shands Stoltzfus, *Set Free: A Journey Toward Solidarity Against Racism* (Scottdale, Pa.: Herald Press, 2001), chapter 6, "Continuing the Journey: Dispelling the Myth."

29. Nancy Carlsson-Paige and Diane Levin, *Who's Calling the Shots?: How to Respond Effectively to Children's Fascination with War Play and War Toys* (Gabriola Island, B.C.: New Society Publishers, 1990), 61. See also Daphne White, "Marketing Violence to Our Children," *Parenting for Peace and Justice Newsletter* 92 (May 2001).

30. Carlsson-Paige and Levin, *Who's Calling the Shots?*, 61.

31. Ibid., 64.

32. Jim and Kathleen McGinnis, *Educating for Peace and Justice, Religious Dimensions, K-6*, rev. ed. (St. Louis, Mo.: Institute for Peace and Justice, 1993), has a list of other nonviolent activities that incorporate speed, strength, and motion for children. The Lion and Lamb Project maintains a dirty dozen list of the year's most violent toys and a top twenty list of creative, nonviolent toys on their website, along with a list of books about nonviolent, age-appropriate toys (301-654-3091, www.lionlamb.org). For game companies with creative and cooperative games, check out Family Pastimes' catalog (888-267-4414, www.familypastimes.com), Aristoplay (888-478-4263, www.aristoplay.com), Animal Town Game Co. (800-445-8642, www.animaltown.com), and Discovery Toys (800-426-4777, www.discoverytoysinc.com).

33. Pamela Baldwin-Ford, *Tatterhood and Other Tales: Stories of Magic and Adventure* (New York: Feminist Press, 1989). See other titles in lists on the companion website (http://peace.mennolink.org/teachpeace).

34. The Gideon story is in Judges 7:2-22. The Jericho battle is in Joshua 5:13-6:21. Other books for your own questions about violence in the Old Testament are: Lois Barrett, *The Way God Fights: War and Peace in the Old Testament* (Scottdale, Pa.: Herald Press, 1987). Albert Curry Winn, *Ain't Gonna Study War No More: Biblical Ambiguity and the Abolition of War* (Louisville: Westminster/John Knox Press, 1993). Millard C. Lind, *Yahweh Is a Warrior: The Theology of Warfare in Ancient Israel* (Scottdale, Pa.: Herald Press, 1980). Lois Barrett's book is the easiest reading.

35. Carlsson-Paige and Levin, *Who's Calling the Shots?*, 99.

36. The 1997 Cinderella video by Disney starring Brandy, Paulo Maltebaun, Whoopi Goldberg, and Whitney Houston at least offers a refreshingly multiethnic cast.

37. For strong females: Robert N. Munsch, *The Paper Bag Princess* (Toronto: Firefly Books, 1985). Katherine Paterson, *The King's Equal* (New York: HarperCollins, 1992). Shirley Climo, *A Treasury of Princesses: Princess Tales from Around the World* (New York: HarperCollins, 1996). For nurturing male role models: Molly Garret Brown's pre-school bedtime book with an African-American dad, *Ten, Nine, Eight* (New York: William Morrow, 1983). Susan Thompson, *One More Thing, Dad* (Chicago: Whitman, 1980). Marjorie Barker, *Magical Hands* (New York: Simon & Schuster, 1989). Florence Freedman, *The Brothers: A Hebrew Legend* (New York: HarperCollins, 1985). Jeremy Roberts, *The Real Deal: A Guy's Guide to Being a Guy* (New York: Rosen Publishing Group, 2000). Eve Merriam, *Daddies at Work* and *Mommies at Work* (New York: Simon & Schuster, 1989) give an inclusive view for 4-8 year olds. For more books, see the Annotated Peace Resource List on the companion website (http://peace.mennolink.org/teachpeace), particularly the "Gender Issues" and "Biographies" sections.

38. Kathleen and James McGinnis, *Parenting for Peace and Justice: Ten Years Later*, 85.

39. Michael Rich, American Academy of Pediatrics, Statement before the Public Health Summit on Entertainment Violence, July 26, 2000.

40. David Grossman, "Trained to Kill," *Christianity Today* (10 August 1998): 30. This article gives an excellent overview of the issues.

41. Parents' Television Council.

42. Deborah Roffman cited in Kathleen Kelleher, "Don't Let TV Be the Main Source of Your Teenager's Sex Education," *Los Angeles Times*, 30 April 2001, E2. The website

http://www.bluecorncomics.com/news.htm has, among other things, articles on various negative effects of media.

43. Gordon Houser, "Mediaculture," *The Mennonite* (19 June 2001): 15.

44. Average U.S. video and/or computer playing time each week for teens in 2001 was 9 hours—13 for boys, 5 for girls—according to the National Institute on Media and the Family, 2001. Canadian teens averaged 5 hours per week in 1998, according to the CBC Backgrounder.

45. American Academy of Pediatrics Policy Statement, August 1999.

46. Nielsen Media Research, 2000.

47. U.S. Department of Education, "Strong Families, Strong Schools: Building Community Partnerships for Learning," 1994.

48. American Academy of Pediatrics, cited by National Institute on Media and the Family in "Children and Advertising Fact Sheet," 2000.

49. Senate Judiciary Committee Staff Report, "Children, Violence, and the Media," 1999. More research is presented by the National Institute on Media and the Family at www.mediafamily.org.

50. Statistics Canada and the Canadian Broadcasting Corp. Backgrounder, 2002. For more Canadian facts, visit the Media Awareness Network at www.reseau-medias.ca/eng/issues/stats/usetv.htm.

51. The National Institute on Media and the Family: 888-672-5437, www.mediafamily.org. The Lion & Lamb Project has video game and movie reviews and a list of books about what parents can do to protect children from media violence: www.lionlamb.org. The Coalition for Quality Children's Media has a newsletter and directory for choosing videos and CD's: 505-989-807, www.cqcm.org/kidsfirst. The Center for Media Literacy helps adults and youth use critical thinking skills to evaluate and create media: 800-228-4630, www.medialit.org. A good print resource is Diane E. Levin, *Remote Control Childhood? Combating the Hazards of Media Culture* (Washington D.C.: National Association for the Education of Young Children, 1988).

52. American Academy of Pediatrics (www.aap.org) has various related articles, including "Some Things You Should Know About Media Violence and Media Literacy," (www.aap.org/advocacy/childhealthmonth/media.htm) and "What Parents Can Do About TV," (www.aap.org/advocacy/childhealthmonth/tv-2.htm).

53. TV-Turnoff Network: 202-518-5556, www.tvturnoff.org.

54. In 1996, the Parenting for Peace and Justice Network hosted a national gathering which initiated the Families Against Violence Advocacy Network (FAVAN) and commissioned the Family Pledge of Nonviolence. It also offers a series of resources to help families implement the pledge.

55. Jim McGinnis, *Families Creating a Circle of Peace*. Anne Marie Witchger Hansen and Susan Vogt, *Kids Creating Circles of Peace* (St. Louis: Institute for Peace and Justice, 2000). Both are available from the Institute for Peace and Justice, see page 70.

Chapter 5

1. Helen Keller in *Alternatives' Spirit of Simplicity* (Sioux City, Iowa: Alternatives, 2002).

2. Maps with the Peters projection show more accurate land areas than the traditional Mercator projection.

3. Mennonite Central Committee (MCC): see page 70 for contact information.

4. *National Geographic, National Geographic World* (for children), and MCC's *A Common Place* (888-563-4676, acp@mcc.org, www.mcc.org/acp) provide excellent articles and photos of world cultures. *New Internationalist* (905-946-0407, magazines@indas.on.ca) from the United Kingdom, provides colorful coverage of global justice issues.

5. AI USA: Freedom Writer's Network (212-807-8400, www.amnestyusa.org), Urgent Action Network: (www.amnestyusa.org/urgent/newslett.html), AIKids (www.amnestyusa.org/aikids/ceua). AI Canada: Urgent Action Network: (416-363-9933, www.amnesty.ca/urgentaction/index.html), Youth and student (www.amnesty.ca/youth/index.html).

6. Europa Pages is an international language school with a monitored site for students to exchange contact information: www.europa-pages.com/penpal_form.html. UNICEF's Voices of Youth website hosts a meeting place and other pages to connect youth with international situations:

www.unicef.org/voy/meeting/meethome.html. The site conforms to the Children's Online Privacy Protection Act of 1998, COPPA.

7. Mathis Wackernagel, "Ecological Footprints of Nations: How Much Nature Do They Use? How Much Nature Do They Have?" www.ecouncil.ac.cr/rio/focus/report/english/footprint/ranking.htm. David Schrock-Shenk ed., *Basic Trek: Venture into a World of Enough, the Original 28-Day Journey* (Scottdale, Pa.: Herald Press, 2002), 77-81, gives slightly older and lower figures.

8. See resources in note 14 of chapter 4.

9. Philip Yancey, *Soul Survivor* (New York: Doubleday, 2001), 202.

10. Florence Perry Heide and Judith Heide Gilliland, *Sami and the Time of Troubles* (New York: Clarion, 1992).

11. Deuteronomy 6:5-7.

12. Mark 12:31.

Chapter 6

1. Doris Janzen Longacre in *Alternatives' Spirit of Simplicity* (Sioux City, Iowa: Alternatives, 2002).

2. Diane Stanley, *Rumpelstiltskin's Daughter* (New York: William Morrow, 1997). Dr. Seuss, *The Butter Battle Book* (New York: Random House,1984).

3. On the early church's participation in war, see John Driver, *How Christians Made Peace with War: Early Christian Understandings of War* (Scottdale, Pa.: Herald Press, 1988). Another, more difficult book, is Jean-Michel Hornus, *It Is Not Lawful for Me to Fight: Early Christian Attitudes Toward War, Violence, and the State*, rev. ed. (Scottdale, Pa.: Herald Press, 1980). You can find useful material to share with youth in Susan Mark Landis, *But Why Don't We Go to War?* (Scottdale, Pa.: Herald Press, 1993).

4. For Christian Peacemaker Form information: www.mcc.org/ask-a-vet/peacemaker.html. For other youth peace information and resources, see the Mennonite Peace and Justice Support Network site: www.peace.mennonlink.org/youth.html.

5. Both of these are available from MCC: see page 70 for contact information.

6. Atlee Beechy, *Seeking Peace: My Journey* (Goshen, Ind.: Pinchpenny Press, 2001), 206.

Resources for the journey

Companion Website: http://peace.mennolink.org/teachpeace

This site includes:
• Annotated Peace Resource List: Books, Videos, Music, Websites for All Ages, a large list of resources for ages 3 to adult compiled by the author. You can search them by subject, format, or age group.
• Links to many other peace resource lists and peace organizations
• Conflict response surveys (for grades 3-5, 6-8, 9-12, and adult)
• Peace Reader Program forms

Parent Resources:

Alternatives for Simple Living. *Treasury of Celebrations: Create Celebrations That Reflect Your Values and Don't Cost the Earth.* Carolyn Pogue, ed. Canada: Northstone, 1997.

Aschliman, Kathryn. *Growing Toward Peace: Stories from Teachers and Parents About Real Children Learning to Live Peacefully.* Scottdale, Pa.: Herald Press, 1993.

Berlowe, Burt, Elizabeth Lonning, and Joseph Cress. *The Peaceful Parenting Handbook.* San Jose, Calif.: Resource Publications, 2001.

Break Forth into Joy! Beyond a Consumer Lifestyle video. Produced by Burst Video Film, Inc. Sioux City, IA: Alternatives for Simple Living, 1995. Videocassette. Full transcript is on the web: (www.simpleliving.org/Archives/VideoScripts/BreakforthJoy.html).

Carlsson-Paige, Nancy, and Diane Levin. *Who's Calling the Shots?: How to Respond Effectively to Children's Fascination with War Play and War Toys.* Gabriola Island, B.C.: New Society Publishers, 1990.

Cecil, Nancy Lee, with Patricia L. Roberts. *Raising Peaceful Children in a Violent World.* San Diego, Calif.: LuraMedia, 1995.

Crary, Elizabeth. *Pick Up Your Socks:. . . And Other Skills Growing Children Need!: A Practical Guide to Raising Responsible Children.* Seattle: Parenting Press, 1990.

Dawn, Marva J. *Keeping the Sabbath Wholly: Ceasing, Resting, Embracing, Feasting.* Grand Rapids, Mich.: Eerdmans, 1989.

de Leon-Hartshorn, Iris, Tobin Miller Shearer, and Regina Shands Stoltzfus. *Set Free: A Journey Toward Solidarity Against Racism.* Scottdale, Pa.: Herald Press, 2001.

Faber, Adele, and Elaine Mazlish. *Siblings without Rivalry: How to Help Your Children Live Together So You Can Live Too.* New York: William Morrow, 1998.

Jantzi, Jeanne Zimmerly. *Parent Trek: Nurturing Creativity and Care in Our Children.* Scottdale, Pa.: Herald Press, 2001.

Juhnke, James, and Carol Hunter. *The Missing Peace: The Search for Nonviolent Alternatives in United States History.* Waterloo: Pandora Press, 2001.

Landis, Susan Mark. *But Why Don't We Go to War?: Finding Jesus' Path to Peace.* Scottdale, Pa.: Herald Press, 1993.

Longacre, Doris Janzen, et al. *Living More with Less.* Scottdale, Pa.: Herald Press, 1980.

Mathias, Barbara, and Mary Ann French. *40 Ways to Raise a Nonracist Child.* New York: HarperCollins, 1996.

McGinnis, James, et al. *Families Creating a Circle of Peace: A Guide for Living the Family*

Pledge of Nonviolence. St. Louis: Families Against Violence Advocacy Network, 1996.

McGinnis, Kathleen and James. *Parenting for Peace and Justice: Ten Years Later.* New York: Orbis Books, 1990.

Muller, Wayne. *Sabbath: Restoring the Sacred Rhythm of Rest.* New York: Random House, 1999.

Nelsen, Jane, Lynn Lott, and H. Stephen Glenn. *Positive Discipline A-Z: 1001 Solutions for Everyday Parenting Problems.* 2d ed. Rocklin, Calif.: Prima, 1999.

Robinson, Jo, and Jean Coppock Staeheli. *Unplug the Christmas Machine.* Rev. ed. New York: William Morrow, 1991.

Schrock-Shenk, David, ed. *Basic Trek: Venture into a World of Enough: The Original 28-Day Journey.* Scottdale, Pa.: Herald Press, 2002.

Sheard, Murray. *Living Simply: Studies in Learning to Live as Jesus Did.* Auckland: World Vision of New Zealand, 1999. (Available from Alternatives: see page 69).

Sider, Ronald J. *Rich Christians in an Age of Hunger: Moving from Affluence to Generosity.* Dallas: Word Publishing, 1997.

Children-Youth Resources:

Baldwin-Ford, Pamela. *Tatterhood and Other Tales: Stories of Magic and Adventure.* New York: Feminist Press, 1989. (Ages 9-12)

Baylor, Byrd. *The Table Where Rich People Sit.* New York: Atheneum, 1994. (Ages 6-adult)

Bosch, Carl W. *Bully on the Bus.* Seattle: Parenting Press, 1988. (Ages 7-11) See others in The Decision Is Yours series.

Colman, Penny. *Girls: A History of Growing Up Female in America.* New York: Scholastic, 2000. (Ages 11-adult)

Crary, Elizabeth. *I Want to Play.* 2d ed. Seattle: Parenting Press, 1996. (Ages 4-8). See others in the Children's Problem Solving series.

Freedman, Florence. *The Brothers: A Hebrew Legend.* New York: HarperCollins, 1985. (Ages 5-9)

Hearne, Betsy. *Seven Brave Women.* New York: Greenwillow, 1997. (Ages 5-9)

Heide, Florence Parry and Judith Heide Gilliland. *Sami and the Time of Troubles.* New York: Clarion, 1992. (Ages 6-10)

Kissinger, Katie. *All the Colors We Are: The Story of How We Get Our Skin Color / Todos los Colores de Nuestra Piel.* St. Paul, Minn.: RedLeaf, 1994. (Ages 4-8)

Lachner, Dorothea. *Andrew's Angry Words.* New York: North-South Books, 1997. (Ages 4-7)

Loewen, James W. *Lies My Teacher Told Me: Everything Your American History Textbook Got Wrong.* New York: Touchstone, 1996. (Ages 12-adult)

Merriam, Eve. *Daddies at Work.* New York: Simon & Schuster, 1989. (Ages 4-8)
_____. *Mommies at Work.* New York: Simon & Schuster, 1989. (Ages 4-8)

Millman, Dan and T. Taylor Bruce. *Secret of the Peaceful Warrior: A Story About Courage and Love.* Tiburon, Calif.: H. J. Kramer, 1991. (Ages 5-9)

Naylor, Phyllis Reynolds. *The King of the Playground.* New York: Simon & Schuster, 1994. (Ages 4-7)

Paterson, Katherine. *The King's Equal.* New York: HarperCollins, 1992. (Ages 7-10)

Roberts, Jeremy. *The Real Deal: A Guy's Guide to Being a Guy.* New York: Rosen Publishing Group, 2000. (Ages 9-12)

Schmidt, Fran and Alice Friedman. *Creative Conflict Solving for Kids*. Miami: Grace Contrino Abrams Peace Education Foundation, 1991. (Similar titles available for different elementary grades.)

Scholes, Katherine. *Peace Begins with You*. San Francisco: Sierra Club Books, 1990. (Ages 5-9)

Seuss, Dr. *The Butter Battle Book*. New York: Random House, 1984. (Ages 5-9)

Simon, Norma. *I Was So Mad!* Morton Grove, Ill.: Albert Whitman, 1974. (Ages 4-7)

Stanley, Diane. *Rumpelstiltskin's Daughter*. New York: William Morrow, 1997. (Ages 5-adult)

Vigna, Judith. *Anyhow, I'm Glad I Tried*. New York: Albert Whitman, 1978. (Ages 4-8)

Wilde, Jerry. *Hot Stuff to Help Kids Chill Out: The Anger Management Book*. Richmond, Ind.: LGR Publishing, 1997. (Ages 8-12)

Organizations:

Alternatives for Simple Living
800-821-6153; PO Box 2787, Sioux City, IA 51106; www.SimpleLiving.org
Books, games, resources on celebrations, Christmas, consumerism. The mission of Alternatives for Simple Living is "to equip people of faith to challenge consumerism, live justly, and celebrate responsibly."

Baptist Peace Fellowship of North America
704-521-6051; 4800 Wedgewood Dr., Charlotte, NC 28210; www.bpfna.org
Books, newsletter, congregational resources, bookmarks.

Buy Nothing Christmas
604-730-9480; www.buynothingchristmas.org
A national initiative started by Canadian Mennonites in 2001 that offers ways to say "No" to conspicuous consumption and "Yes" to true abundance at Christmas.

Celebrating Peace
www.celebratingpeace.com
Resources and program ideas. Site includes the Visions of Peace Art Collection.

Coalition for Quality Children's Media
505-989-8076; www.cqcm.org/kidsfirst
A collaboration of media industry companies, educators, child advocacy organizations, and families. Their mission is to teach children critical viewing skills and increase the visibility and availability of quality children's programs. **KIDS FIRST!** is the Coalition's program that evaluates and rates children's films, videos, DVDs, audio recordings, software, and television programs.

Educators for Social Responsibility
800-370-2515; 23 Garden St., Cambridge, MA 02138; www.esrnational.org
ESR's mission is to make teaching social responsibility a core practice in education.

A Force More Powerful
www.pbs.org/weta/forcemorepowerful/
Developed to support the PBS documentary "A Force More Powerful," there is also an accompanying book with the same title. The website shares background information on the film and 13 specific historical examples. It discusses what nonviolent action is, and what it is *not*: passive, only for saints, dependent on the good will of others, etc.

The Institute for Peace and Justice

314-533-4445; 4144 Lindell Blvd. #408, St. Louis, MO 63108; www.ipj-ppj.org

Founded and led by Jim and Kathleen McGinnis, this includes the Parenting for Peace and Justice Network (PPJN), an interfaith, interracial, transnational association of families of all descriptions who seek shalom. Families Against Violence Advocacy Network (FAVAN), a broadly-based network for violence prevention in families, schools parishes, congregations, colleges, and prisons, is also part of the Institute. The centerpiece of FAVAN is the Family Pledge of Nonviolence, available at www.ipj-ppj.org/pledge.html.

The Lion and the Lamb Project

http://lionlamb.org

This provides toy and movie ratings and book lists.

Mennonite Central Committee (MCC) Canada

888-622-6337; 134 Plaza Dr., Winnipeg, MB R3T 5K9; www.mcc.org

Mennonite Central Committee (MCC) U.S.

888-563-4676; 21 S. 12th St., PO Box 500, Akron, PA 17501; www.mcc.org

The MCC Resource Catalog is available on the web: www.mcc.org/respub.html.

Mennonite Missions Network's Third Way Café

http://thirdway.com/peace/

Peace Blend pages include an introduction to the Mennonite denomination and its peace position, stories of current peacemakers, essays on current events, peacemaking activities, answers to questions, and more.

Mennonite Peace and Justice Support Network, Mennonite Church USA

866-866-2872; http://peacemennolink.org/teachpeace

A program of Mennonite Church USA, this website includes many worship and action resources, as well as useful links.

The National Institute on Media and the Family

800-672-5437; www.mediafamily.org

A national resource for those interested in the influence of electronic media on children. Resources include movie, television, and video game content ratings.

Parenting Press

800-992-6657; www.parentingpress.com

Their goal is to offer useful books that teach practical life skills to children (like problem solving, conflict resolution, and acknowledging and dealing with feelings) and those who care for them (effective tools for guiding, disciplining, and caring for children).

Peace Education Foundation

800-749-8838; www.PeaceEducation.com

They publish PeaceWorks curricula for grades K-12, some in Spanish. They also carry resources for pre-schoolers and parents, and cooperative games for groups.

TV-Turnoff Network

800-939-6737; www.tvturnoff.org.

This organization has provided many resources for a TV-Turnoff Week each April since 1994.

About the Author

Anne Meyer Byler has been involved in peace and justice activities as an activist, organizer, and writer. She holds degrees in peace studies and library science and has particular interest in promoting peacemaking resources. Anne and her husband, Mark, are members of Assembly Mennonite Church in Goshen, Indiana. Their recent experiences in parenting a teen, preteen, and active preschooler have grounded Anne's parenting ideas in the practical.

With consumerism and violence escalating all around us, even dedicated parents wonder how to help their children cope with it all. *How to Teach Peace to Children* provides so many helpful suggestions for families and for our society as a whole

—James & Kathleen McGinnis, Directors of the Institute for Peace and Justice and International Coordinators for the Parenting for Peace and Justice Network.

We all raise children, whether they live with us or not. Make this book your baby-shower gift, your reference during times of community or national upheaval, your Sunday school lesson, your sermon reference.
—Susan Mark Landis, Peace Advocate, Mennonite Church USA

As the mother of a young child, I found *How to Teach Peace to Children* to be a helpful, realistic, and compassionate guide to the challenges and joys of raising a peaceful child. Byler tells stories of adult and child foibles and mistakes (often with a good dose of humor) even while holding up a vision of how we can all become more and more the people God has created us to be.
—LeDayne McLeese Polaski, Managing Director,
Baptist Peace Fellowship of North America

As a mother and a pastor I strongly believe that our future may depend on our walking with, and learning from, the child-like peacemakers among us. Anne Meyer Byler has given us a gift that invites us to honesty, growth, change and a hope-filled future. Dare to join her!
—Carmen Schrock-Hurst, Pastor, Mennonite Church USA

How to Teach Peace to Children is an important tool for families and congregations who are committed to being and raising peacemakers. This slim little book contains a real wealth of positive steps for families to consider as they strive to understand peace, family dynamics, our relationships with others, walking the talk, learn about our global village, and partner with their congregations in nurturing the faith of their children.
—Elsie Rempel, Christian Education and Nurture,
Mennonite Church Canada